Mastering C++ Network Automation

AF574649

Run Automation across Configuration Management, Container Orchestration, Kubernetes, and Cloud Networking

Justin Barbara

Copyright © 2023 by GitforGits.

All rights reserved. This book is protected under copyright laws and no part of it may be reproduced or transmitted in any form or by any means, electronic or mechanical, including photocopying, recording, or by any information storage and retrieval system, without the prior written permission of the publisher. Any unauthorized reproduction, distribution, or transmission of this work may result in civil and criminal penalties and will be dealt with in the respective jurisdiction at anywhere in India, in accordance with the applicable copyright laws.

Published by: GitforGits
Publisher: Sonal Dhandre
www.gitforgits.com
support@gitforgits.com

Printed in India

First Printing: March 2023

ISBN: 978-8196228569

Cover Design by: Kitten Publishing

For permission to use material from this book, please contact GitforGits at support@GitforGits.com.

Content

Preface

This book is an in-depth guide for network administrators, cloud architects, and container and Kubernetes administrators who want to learn how to automate networking tasks in C++. From setting up a network automation environment to automating configuration management and working with containers and container orchestration tools such as Kubernetes, the book covers a wide range of topics.

The first section of the book covers the fundamentals of automation scripting and testing. Readers will learn how to create successful automation scripts and test them to ensure they perform properly. The next section describes how to set up a network automation environment. This includes configuring network devices, servers, and other components required for automation. The readers will learn about the various protocols as well as how to use Ansible to automate the configuration management of these devices. It covers containerization and container orchestration systems such as Docker and Kubernetes. Readers will learn how to use tools such as Docker Compose and Kubernetes to automate workload management and deployment.

The final section of the book focuses on cloud networking. The readers will learn how to handle network resources in cloud systems such as AWS, Google Cloud, and Azure. Readers get to work with tools and services available for cloud networking automation and how to use them in their regular cloud networking operations.

In this book you will learn how to:

- Setting up GNS3, Eclipse IDE, cpp-netlib, Boost, OpenSSL, and zlib libraries
- Configure the ports, hosts, and servers using C++ scripting
- Writing, testing, and validating network automation scripts in both, test and production environment
- Building docker images, running containers, and managing container deployments
- Using Ansible for server provisioning, automated system identification and managing auto-updates
- Automating container scheduling, service discovery, and load balancing
- Setting up Kubernetes cluster, Nginx ingress, implementing service mesh, and automating firewall configuration
- Working with AWS, Azure and Google Cloud Networking Services for Cloud Automation

GitforGits

Prerequisites

This is a fantastic desk reference for network administrators, cloud architects, devops engineers, automation engineers wishing to automate networking tasks with C++. It is a must-have book for anyone who wants to keep ahead of the curve in the field of networking automation.

Codes Usage

Are you in need of some helpful code examples to assist you in your programming and documentation? Look no further! Our book offers a wealth of supplemental material, including code examples and exercises.

Not only is this book here to aid you in getting your job done, but you have our permission to use the example code in your programs and documentation. However, please note that if you are reproducing a significant portion of the code, we do require you to contact us for permission.

But don't worry, using several chunks of code from this book in your program or answering a question by citing our book and quoting example code does not require permission. But if you do choose to give credit, an attribution typically includes the title, author, publisher, and ISBN. For example, "Mastering C++ Network Automation by Justin Barbara".

If you are unsure whether your intended use of the code examples falls under fair use or the permissions outlined above, please do not hesitate to reach out to us at support@gitforgits.com.

We are happy to assist and clarify any concerns.

Acknowledgement

I owe a tremendous debt of gratitude to GitforGits, for their unflagging enthusiasm and wise counsel throughout the entire process of writing this book. Their knowledge and careful editing helped make sure the piece was useful for people of all reading levels and comprehension skills. In addition, I'd like to thank everyone involved in the publishing process for their efforts in making this book a reality. Their efforts, from copyediting to advertising, made the project what it is today.

Finally, I'd like to express my gratitude to everyone who has shown me unconditional love and encouragement throughout my life. Their support was crucial to the completion of this book. I appreciate your help with this endeavour and your continued interest in my career.

CHAPTER 1: C++ BASICS FOR NETWORKS

Capability of C++ for Networks

Overview

C++ is a popular programming language that is widely used for developing network-based applications, including network programming and network automation. C++ provides a rich set of features and libraries that make it easy to develop complex network applications that can run on various operating systems and hardware platforms. In this section, we will discuss the concept of ease of C++ for network programming and network automation.

C++ is a high-level programming language that allows developers to write code in a more structured and object-oriented way. C++ has a rich set of libraries that make it easy to develop network-based applications. The standard library of C++ provides a set of classes and functions that allow developers to write network applications quickly and easily. These libraries include socket programming, threading, and concurrency. C++ also provides a variety of libraries, such as Boost.Asio, that offer advanced features for network programming.

Why C++ for Networks?

One of the significant benefits of using C++ for network programming is its low-level access to the operating system. C++ provides direct access to system-level APIs, which allows developers to develop efficient and high-performance network applications. C++ supports low-level socket programming, which is essential for developing network applications that require high-performance and low latency.

C++ is also a highly portable language that can be used on various platforms. This means that network applications developed in C++ can run on multiple platforms, including Windows, Linux, and macOS. The portability of C++ is due to its compatibility with different operating systems and hardware architectures. This feature makes C++ an ideal choice for developing cross-platform network applications.

C++ also provides robust support for multithreading, which is essential for developing high-performance network applications. Multithreading allows developers to write applications that can handle multiple connections simultaneously. This is important for network applications that require high throughput and low latency. C++ also provides libraries like std::thread that allow developers to write multithreaded applications quickly and easily.

In addition to network programming, C++ is also a suitable language for network automation. Network automation involves automating repetitive network-related tasks, such as configuration management, monitoring, and testing. C++ provides a wide range of libraries and tools that can be used for network automation. For example, C++ provides libraries like Boost.PropertyTree that allow developers to read and write configuration files easily. C++ also provides tools like Boost.Test that allow developers to write automated tests for network applications.

C++ also provides robust support for object-oriented programming (OOP). OOP is essential for developing large and complex network applications. OOP allows developers to break down an application into smaller, more manageable parts. This makes it easier to maintain and modify the code over time. C++ also provides advanced features like templates and generic programming, which allow developers to write generic algorithms that can be used with different data types.

Another advantage of using C++ for network programming and network automation is the large community of developers and users. C++ has a vast community of developers who share their knowledge and expertise through forums, blogs, and open-source projects. This community provides a rich source of knowledge and resources that can be used to develop network applications and automate network-related tasks.

C++ is a popular programming language that is widely used for network programming and network automation. C++ provides a rich set of libraries and tools that make it easy to develop network-based applications that can run on various platforms. C++ provides low-level access to the operating system, which allows developers to write efficient and high-performance network applications. C++ also provides robust support for multithreading, object-oriented programming, and generic programming, which are essential for developing complex network applications. The large community of developers and users is also a significant advantage of using C++ for network programming and network automation.

Data Types of C++

C++ is a powerful and versatile programming language that provides a rich set of data types to represent different kinds of data. These data types allow developers to define variables, constants, and other data structures in their code. In this section, we will discuss each of the data types available in C++, along with their characteristics, examples, and use cases.

Boolean Data Type

The Boolean data type in C++ represents a value that is either true or false. It is used to store binary values, such as the result of a comparison or a logical operation. The Boolean data type is declared using the bool keyword.

Example:

```
bool is_true = true;
bool is_false = false;
```

Character Data Type

The character data type in C++ represents a single character. It is used to store letters, digits, and special characters. The character data type is declared using the char keyword.

Example:

```
char letter = 'a';
```

C++ also supports wide characters, which are used to represent characters in different languages. Wide characters are declared using the wchar_t keyword.

Example:

```
wchar_t chinese_char = L'中';
```

Integer Data Types

The integer data types in C++ represent whole numbers. There are several different integer data types available in C++, each with different ranges and sizes. The most commonly used integer data types are:

Int

This data type represents signed integers and has a range of -2,147,483,648 to 2,147,483,647. It is declared using the int keyword.

Example:

```
int number = 42;
```

Long

This data type represents signed long integers and has a range of -9,223,372,036,854,775,808 to 9,223,372,036,854,775,807. It is declared using the long keyword.

Example:

```
long big_number = 1234567890;
```

Short

This data type represents signed short integers and has a range of -32,768 to 32,767. It is declared using the short keyword.

Example:

```
short small_number = 42;
```

unsigned int

This data type represents unsigned integers and has a range of 0 to 4,294,967,295. It is declared using the unsigned int keyword.

Example:

```
unsigned int positive_number = 42;
```

Floating-Point Data Types

The floating-point data types in C++ represent real numbers with a fractional part. There are two floating-point data types available in C++:

Float

This data type represents single-precision floating-point numbers and has a range of approximately 1.2E-38 to 3.4E+38. It is declared using the float keyword.

Example:

```
float number = 3.14;
```

Double

This data type represents double-precision floating-point numbers and has a range of approximately 2.2E-308 to 1.8E+308. It is declared using the double keyword.

Example:

```
double big_number = 1.23456789;
```

Void Data Type

The void data type in C++ is used to indicate that a function does not return any value. It is also used to indicate that a pointer does not point to any data type. The void data type is declared using the void keyword.

Example:

```
void print_message() {
   cout << "Hello World!" << endl;
}
```

Enumeration Data Type

The enumeration data type in C++ is used to define a set of named constants. Each constant in the enumeration is assigned an integer value. The enumeration data type is declared using the enum keyword.

Example:

```
enum Color { Red, Green, Blue };
```

In the above sample program, the enumeration data type Color is defined with three named constants: Red, Green, and Blue. The constants are assigned values 0, 1, and 2, respectively.

Pointer Data Type

The pointer data type in C++ is used to store the memory address of a variable. Pointers are used to manipulate memory directly and to create dynamic data structures such as linked lists and trees. Pointers are declared using the * symbol.

Example:

```
int number = 42;
int* pointer_to_number = &number;
```

In the above given sample program, a pointer called pointer_to_number is declared and assigned the memory address of the integer variable number.

Array Data Type

The array data type in C++ is used to store a collection of elements of the same data type. Arrays are declared using square brackets [].

Example:

```
int numbers[5] = {1, 2, 3, 4, 5};
```

In the above given sample program, an integer array called numbers is declared with 5 elements.

Structure Data Type

The structure data type in C++ is used to define a custom data type that can hold multiple values of different data types. Structures are declared using the struct keyword.

Example:

```
struct Person {
   string name;
   int age;
};

Person person1 = {"John Doe", 30};
```

In the above given sample program, a structure called Person is defined with two member variables: name (a string) and age (an integer). An instance of the structure called person1 is declared and initialized with a name and an age.

Union Data Type

The union data type in C++ is used to define a custom data type that can hold one value of several different data types. Unions are declared using the union keyword.

Example:

```
union Number {
    int i;
    float f;
};

Number number1;
number1.i = 42;
```

In the above given sample program, a union called Number is defined with two member variables: i (an integer) and f (a float). An instance of the union called number1 is declared and assigned an integer value.

To summarize, C++ provides a rich set of data types that allow developers to represent a wide range of data in their code. By understanding the characteristics, examples, and use cases of each data type, developers can choose the most appropriate data type for their specific needs.

C++ Loops

Loops in C++ are used to execute a block of code repeatedly until a certain condition is met. There are three types of loops in C++: for, while, and do-while. In this section, we will discuss the concept and practical usage of each type of loop with examples.

For Loop

The for loop in C++ is used to iterate over a sequence of values. It has three parts: initialization, condition, and update. The initialization part is executed only once at the beginning of the loop. The condition part is checked before each iteration of the loop. If the condition is true, the loop body is executed. The update part is executed at the end of each iteration.
Example:

```
for (int i = 0; i < 5; i++) {
  cout << i << endl;
}
```

In the above given sample program, the for loop iterates from 0 to 4 (inclusive) and prints the value of i in each iteration.

While Loop

The while loop in C++ is used to execute a block of code repeatedly while a certain condition is true. The condition is checked at the beginning of each iteration.

Example:

```
int i = 0;
while (i < 5) {
  cout << i << endl;
  i++;
}
```

In the above given sample program, the while loop iterates from 0 to 4 (inclusive) and prints the value of i in each iteration.

Do-While Loop

The do-while loop in C++ is similar to the while loop, except that the condition is checked at the end of each iteration. This means that the loop body is executed at least once, even if the condition is false.

Example:

```
int i = 0;
do {
  cout << i << endl;
  i++;
} while (i < 5);
```

In the above given sample program, the do-while loop iterates from 0 to 4 (inclusive) and prints the value of i in each iteration.

Loop Control Statements

Loop control statements are used to alter the flow of a loop. There are three types of loop control statements in C++: break, continue, and goto.

Break

The break statement is used to exit a loop prematurely. When a break statement is encountered inside a loop, the loop is immediately terminated, and the program execution continues with the next statement after the loop.

Example:

```
for (int i = 0; i < 10; i++) {
   if (i == 5) {
      break;
   }
   cout << i << endl;
}
```

In the above given sample program, the for loop iterates from 0 to 9 (inclusive), but when i equals 5, the break statement is executed, and the loop is terminated.

Continue

The continue statement is used to skip an iteration of a loop. When a continue statement is encountered inside a loop, the current iteration is skipped, and the program execution continues with the next iteration of the loop.

Example:

```
for (int i = 0; i < 10; i++) {
   if (i == 5) {
      continue;
   }
   cout << i << endl;
```

```
}
```

In the above given sample program, the for loop iterates from 0 to 9 (inclusive), but when i equals 5, the continue statement is executed, and the loop skips the iteration for i=5.

Goto

The goto statement is used to transfer control to a labeled statement in the program. It is considered a harmful statement and should be avoided whenever possible.

Example:

```
int i = 0;
start:
cout << i << endl;
i++;
if (i < 5
{
goto start;
}
```

In the above given sample program, the program jumps to the "start" label using the goto statement. This causes an infinite loop, as the value of i is never greater than or equal to 5.

Nested Loops

Nested loops are loops that are placed inside another loop. They are useful for iterating over multi-dimensional arrays and other complex data structures.

Example:

```
int arr[3][3] = {{1, 2, 3}, {4, 5, 6}, {7, 8, 9}};
for (int i = 0; i < 3; i++) {
for (int j = 0; j < 3; j++) {
cout << arr[i][j] << " ";
}
```

```
cout << endl;
}
```

In the above given sample program, we have a two-dimensional array "arr" with dimensions 3x3. We use a nested for loop to iterate over each element in the array and print its value.

To conclude, Loops are an important concept in C++ programming, and they are used extensively in various applications. In this section, we discussed the three types of loops in C++ (for, while, and do-while) and their practical usage with examples. We also discussed loop control statements (break, continue, and goto) and their usage. Finally, we discussed nested loops and their usage for iterating over multi-dimensional arrays and other complex data structures.

Functions in C++

Functions in C++ are used to group a set of statements together and perform a specific task. They are an important concept in C++ programming, as they help to modularize code and make it more manageable. In this section, we will discuss the concept and practical usage of functions in C++ with examples.

Defining a Function

A function in C++ has a name, a return type, a set of parameters, and a body. The name of a function should be descriptive and give an idea of what the function does. The return type of a function is the data type of the value that the function returns. The parameters of a function are the input values that the function receives, and the body of the function is the set of statements that perform a specific task.

Example:

```
int add(int a, int b) {
   return a + b;
}
```

In the above given sample program, we define a function called "add" that takes two integer parameters (a and b) and returns their sum.

Calling a Function

To use a function in C++, we need to call it. To call a function, we simply write the name of the function followed by a set of parentheses. If the function takes parameters, we pass them inside the parentheses.

Example:

```
int result = add(3, 4);
cout << result << endl;
```

In the above given sample program, we call the "add" function with parameters 3 and 4, and store the result in a variable called "result". We then print the value of "result" to the console.

Default Parameters

In C++, we can set default values for function parameters. This means that if a parameter is not passed to a function, it will use its default value. This can make the function more flexible and easier to use.

Example:

```
int multiply(int a, int b = 2) {
  return a * b;
}
```

In the above given sample program, we define a function called "multiply" that takes two integer parameters (a and b). The default value of b is 2. This means that if we call the function with only one parameter, it will use 2 as the value of b.

```
int result1 = multiply(3, 4);
int result2 = multiply(3);
cout << result1 << endl; // prints 12
cout << result2 << endl; // prints 6
```

In the above given sample program, we call the "multiply" function with two parameters

(3 and 4), and store the result in a variable called "result1". We then call the function with only one parameter (3), and store the result in a variable called "result2". We print both results to the console.

Function Overloading

Function overloading is a feature in C++ that allows us to define multiple functions with the same name but different parameter lists. This can be useful when we want to perform similar tasks with different types of data.

Example:

```
int add(int a, int b) {
  return a + b;
}

double add(double a, double b) {
  return a + b;
}
```

In the above given sample program, we define two functions called "add" that take different parameter types (int and double). This allows us to use the same function name for different types of data.

```
int result1 = add(3, 4);
double result2 = add(3.5, 4.5);
cout << result1 << endl; // prints 7
cout << result2 << endl; // prints 8.0
```

In the above given sample program, we call the "add" function with different parameter types (int and double), and store the results in variables. We print both results to the console.

Recursive Functions

A recursive function is a function that calls itself. This can be useful when we want to perform a task repeatedly with slightly different input values.

Example:

```
int factorial(int n) {
  if (n == 0) {
    return 1;
  } else {
    return n * factorial(n-1);
  }
}
```

In the above given sample program, we define a function called "factorial" that calculates the factorial of a given integer using recursion. The factorial of a number is the product of all positive integers up to that number. For example, the factorial of 4 is 4 * 3 * 2 * 1 = 24.

```
int result = factorial(4);
cout << result << endl; // prints 24
```

In the above given sample program, we call the "factorial" function with the parameter 4, and store the result in a variable called "result". We print the value of "result" to the console.

Passing Arrays to Functions

In C++, we can pass arrays to functions as parameters. This allows us to perform operations on arrays using functions.

Example:

```
void printArray(int arr[], int size) {
  for (int i = 0; i < size; i++) {
    cout << arr[i] << " ";
  }
  cout << endl;
}
```

In the above given sample program, we define a function called "printArray" that takes an array of integers and its size as parameters. The function then iterates over the array and prints each element to the console.

```
int arr[] = {1, 2, 3, 4, 5};
printArray(arr, 5);
```

In the above given sample program, we define an array of integers called "arr" with size 5. We then call the "printArray" function with the array and its size as parameters. The function prints the values of the array to the console.

Overall, Functions are an important concept in C++ programming, as they allow us to modularize code and perform specific tasks. In this section, we discussed the concept of functions in C++ and their practical usage with examples. We discussed defining a function, calling a function, default parameters, function overloading, recursive functions, and passing arrays to functions.

CHAPTER 2: C++ ADVANCED FOR NETWORKS

C++ File Handling

File handling is an important concept in C++ programming that allows us to read and write data to and from files on the computer's hard drive. In this section, we will discuss the concept of file handling in C++ and its practical usage with examples.

File I/O Operations

File Input/Output (I/O) operations in C++ involve reading data from and writing data to files. The C++ Standard Library provides several classes and functions that allow us to perform these operations.

The main classes used for file I/O operations are ifstream and ofstream.

- ifstream: The ifstream class is used to read data from a file.
- ofstream: The ofstream class is used to write data to a file.

Opening File

Before we can read or write data to a file, we need to open the file using the ifstream or ofstream class.

We can open a file in one of the following modes:

- ios::in: Open the file for reading.
- ios::out: Open the file for writing.
- ios::app: Append to the end of the file.
- ios::trunc: Truncate the file before opening it.

Example of opening a file for writing:

```
#include <iostream>
#include <fstream>

using namespace std;

int main() {
  ofstream outFile;
  outFile.open("output.txt");
```

```
  if (outFile.is_open()) {
    outFile << "Hello World!" << endl;
    outFile.close();
  } else {
    cout << "Unable to open file." << endl;
  }

  return 0;
}
```

In the above given sample program, we create an object of the ofstream class called "outFile". We then use the "open" function to open a file called "output.txt" for writing. If the file is opened successfully, we write the string "Hello World!" to the file using the output stream operator "<<" and close the file using the "close" function. If the file cannot be opened, we print an error message to the console.

Reading Data From File

To read data from a file, we can use the ifstream class. We can use the ">>" operator to read data from a file, similar to how we use it to read data from the console.

Example of reading data from a file:

```
#include <iostream>
#include <fstream>
#include <string>

using namespace std;

int main() {
  ifstream inFile;
  string line;

  inFile.open("input.txt");
```

```
    if (inFile.is_open()) {
        while (getline(inFile, line)) {
            cout << line << endl;
        }
        inFile.close();
    } else {
        cout << "Unable to open file." << endl;
    }

    return 0;
}
```

In the above given sample program, we create an object of the ifstream class called "inFile". We also create a string variable called "line" to store each line of the file. We then use the "open" function to open a file called "input.txt" for reading. If the file is opened successfully, we use a while loop to read each line of the file using the "getline" function, and print it to the console. Finally, we close the file using the "close" function. If the file cannot be opened, we print an error message to the console.

Appending To File

To append data to a file, we can open the file in the "app" mode. This will add any new data to the end of the file, without overwriting the existing data.

Example of appending data to a file:

```
#include <iostream>
#include <fstream>

using namespace std;

int main() {
    ofstream outFile;
    outFile.open("output.txt", ios::app);
```

```
    if (outFile.is_open()) {
        outFile << "This is appended to the file." << endl;
    outFile.close();
} else {
    cout << "Unable to open file." << endl;
}

return 0;
}
```

In the above given sample program, we open the file "output.txt" in the "app" mode using the "ios::app" flag. This will open the file for appending, so any new data we write to the file will be added to the end of the file. We then write the string "This is appended to the file." to the file using the output stream operator "<<" and close the file using the "close" function. If the file cannot be opened, we print an error message to the console.

Truncating a File

To truncate a file, we can open the file in the "trunc" mode. This will delete all the existing data in the file and create a new file.

Example of truncating a file:

```
#include <iostream>
#include <fstream>

using namespace std;

int main() {
ofstream outFile;
outFile.open("output.txt", ios::trunc);
if (outFile.is_open()) {
    outFile << "This is a new file." << endl;
```

```
  outFile.close();
} else {
  cout << "Unable to open file." << endl;
}

return 0;
}
```

In the above given sample program, we open the file "output.txt" in the "trunc" mode using the "ios::trunc" flag. This will delete all the existing data in the file and create a new file. We then write the string "This is a new file." to the file using the output stream operator "<<" and close the file using the "close" function. If the file cannot be opened, we print an error message to the console.

Error Handling

When working with files, it is important to handle errors that may occur while reading or writing data to files. We can use the "fail" function to check if an error has occurred while reading or writing data to a file.

Example of error handling:

```
#include <iostream>
#include <fstream>

using namespace std;

int main() {
ifstream inFile;
int num;

inFile.open("input.txt");

if (inFile.fail()) {
  cout << "Unable to open file." << endl;
```

```
    return 1;
}

while (inFile >> num) {
    cout << num << endl;
}

inFile.close();

return 0;
}
```

In the above given sample program, we create an object of the ifstream class called "inFile". We also create an integer variable called "num" to store the data we read from the file. We then use the "open" function to open a file called "input.txt" for reading. If the file cannot be opened, we print an error message to the console and return from the program using the "return 1" statement. If the file is opened successfully, we use a while loop to read each integer from the file using the ">>" operator and print it to the console. Finally, we close the file using the "close" function.

All we can concluded is that, file handling is an important concept in C++ programming that allows us to read and write data to and from files on the computer's hard drive. The C++ Standard Library provides several classes and functions that allow us to perform file I/O operations. We can use the ifstream and ofstream classes to read and write data to files, respectively. We can open a file in different modes such as "in", "out", "app", or "trunc", depending on the operation we want to perform. It is also important to handle errors that

C++ Modules

Overview

Modules were introduced in C++20 as a new way to organize and manage code in large projects. Modules provide a way to encapsulate and package code into reusable units that can be compiled separately from the rest of the code. This makes it easier to manage dependencies and reduce build times, especially in large projects where there may be a lot of code to compile.

In this section, we will explore the concept of modules in C++, how to create and use them, and some examples to illustrate their usage.

What Are Modules?

Modules are a new feature in C++20 that provide a new way to organize and manage code in large projects. A module is a self-contained unit of code that can be compiled separately from the rest of the code. It encapsulates data, types, and functions into a single unit that can be imported by other modules or translation units.

Modules provide a way to manage dependencies more efficiently by reducing the amount of code that needs to be compiled each time the code is built. This can lead to faster build times and better code organization.

Creating Module

To create a module, we use the "module" keyword followed by the name of the module. Inside the module, we can define types, functions, and data that we want to export to other modules.

Example of a simple module:

```
// Module: example
module example;

int add(int a, int b) {
   return a + b;
}

struct Point {
   int x;
   int y;
};
```

In the above given sample program, we create a module called "example" using the "module" keyword. Inside the module, we define a function called "add" that takes two integer parameters and returns their sum. We also define a struct called "Point" that has two integer members, "x" and "y".

Exporting Symbols

To make a symbol (type, function, or data) available to other modules, we need to export it using the "export" keyword. Exporting a symbol makes it available to other modules that import the current module.

Example of exporting symbols:

```
// Module: example
module example;

export int add(int a, int b) {
  return a + b;
}

export struct Point {
  int x;
  int y;
};
```

In the above given sample program, we export the "add" function and the "Point" struct using the "export" keyword. This makes them available to other modules that import the "example" module.

Importing Module

To use symbols from a module, we need to import it using the "import" keyword followed by the name of the module.

Example of importing a module:

```
// Module: main
import example;

int main() {
  Point p = { 1, 2 };
```

```
    int sum = add(p.x, p.y);
    return 0;
}
```

In the above given sample program, we import the "example" module using the "import" keyword. We then use the "add" function and the "Point" struct from the "example" module in our main function.

Compilation and Linking

When we compile a module, it produces a binary file that contains the compiled code for that module. To use a module, we need to link it with the rest of the code. This is done using the linker, which combines the binary files for all the modules and generates the final executable.

Example of compiling and linking a module:

```
$ g++ -std=c++20 -c example.cpp
$ g++ -std=c++20 -c main.cpp
$ g++ -std=c++20 example.o main.o -o program
```

In the above given sample program, we compile the "example" module and the "main" module separately using the "c++20" flag to enable C++20 features. We then link the object files for both modules using the "example.o" and "main.o" files and create an executable called "program".

Advantages of Modules

There are several advantages of using modules in C++:

- Better organization: Modules provide a better way to organize code, making it easier to manage large projects.
- Faster build times: By reducing the amount of code that needs to be compiled, modules can significantly improve build times, especially in large projects.
- Encapsulation: Modules provide a way to encapsulate code, making it easier to manage dependencies and reduce the risk of name collisions.
- Improved performance: Modules can help improve performance by allowing the compiler to optimize code more effectively.

Overall, modules are a powerful new feature in C++20 that provide a new way to organize and manage code in large projects. They provide a way to encapsulate and package code into reusable units that can be compiled separately from the rest of the code, making it easier to manage dependencies and reduce build times. Modules also provide better organization and encapsulation of code, which can help improve performance and reduce the risk of name collisions. Overall, modules are a valuable addition to C++ that can help developers create better, more efficient code.

My First C++ Script

Following is an example script that incorporates several concepts we've covered in this chapter:

```
#include <iostream>
#include <fstream>
#include <string>
#include <vector>

using namespace std;

// Define a function that takes a vector of integers and returns the sum
int sumVector(vector<int> nums) {
   int sum = 0;
   for (int i = 0; i < nums.size(); i++) {
      sum += nums[i];
   }
   return sum;
}

int main() {
   // Open a file for writing
   ofstream outfile("example.txt");

   // Write some data to the file
```

```
  outfile << "This is some data.\n";
  outfile << "This is some more data.\n";
  outfile.close();

  // Open the file for reading
  ifstream infile("example.txt");

  // Read the contents of the file
  string line;
  while (getline(infile, line)) {
    cout << line << endl;
  }
  infile.close();

  // Create a vector of integers and add some numbers to it
  vector<int> nums;
  nums.push_back(1);
  nums.push_back(2);
  nums.push_back(3);
  nums.push_back(4);
  nums.push_back(5);

  // Compute the sum of the vector using our function
  int sum = sumVector(nums);
  cout << "The sum is: " << sum << endl;

  return 0;
}
```

In the above given sample program, we Include several standard C++ headers, including <iostream> for input/output, <fstream> for file I/O, <string> for string handling, and <vector> for working with dynamic arrays.

Define a function sumVector that takes a vector of integers and returns their sum. In main, we open a file for writing, write some data to it, and then close it. We then open the same file for reading, read its contents line by line, and print them to the console. Finally, we create a vector of integers, add some numbers to it, and compute their sum using our sumVector function.

This example demonstrates how to work with various C++ features we've discussed, including headers, file I/O, functions, and vectors.

Summary

In this chapter, we covered several key concepts and features of the C++ programming language.

We began by discussing the basics of C++ syntax and structure, including the use of comments, variables, and data types. We discussed the difference between primitive data types such as integers, floats, and booleans, and more complex data types like strings, arrays, and structs. We also covered some basic operators and expressions, such as arithmetic operators, comparison operators, and logical operators, and we demonstrated how these could be used to perform calculations and comparisons.

Next, we discussed control structures in C++, including conditional statements (if/else) and loops (for, while, do-while). We demonstrated how these structures could be used to control program flow and execute different parts of the code based on certain conditions. We also discussed the use of break and continue statements to modify loop behavior.

We then covered functions in C++, which are reusable blocks of code that can be called from other parts of the program. We discussed the syntax for defining and calling functions, and we demonstrated how functions could be used to perform specific tasks, such as computing the sum of a vector of integers or generating a Fibonacci sequence.

Next, we discussed file handling in C++, which allows programs to read from and write to external files. We demonstrated how to open and close files, write data to them, and read data from them using streams. We also discussed the importance of error handling when working with files, and we demonstrated how to check for errors and handle them appropriately.

We then covered classes and objects in C++, which are the building blocks of object-oriented programming (OOP). We discussed the basic syntax for defining classes and creating objects from them, and we demonstrated how classes could be used to encapsulate data and behavior and create more complex, modular programs. We used the example of a Rectangle class to demonstrate how to define class attributes, methods, and constructors.

Finally, we discussed modules in C++, which are a newer feature introduced in C++20. Modules allow programs to define self-contained, reusable units of code that can be imported and used by other parts of the program. We discussed the syntax for defining and importing modules, and we demonstrated how modules could be used to simplify program structure and reduce dependencies between different parts of the code.

Throughout the chapter, we provided practical examples and demonstrations of each concept, with the goal of helping you understand the basic syntax and structure of the C++ language and how to use its various features to write functional, efficient, and modular code. By the end of the chapter, you should have a solid foundation in C++ programming and be ready to start exploring more advanced topics and applications of the language.

CHAPTER 3: PREPARING NETWORK AUTOMATION SETUP

Elements of Network Automation Lab

Network automation has become a critical part of modern network management, and it has significantly increased the efficiency and effectiveness of network operations. A network automation lab is a testing environment that simulates a network, allowing engineers to experiment with different configurations and scenarios without impacting the production environment. C++ is a programming language that is widely used in network automation labs due to its performance, flexibility, and robustness. In this section, we will discuss the various components of a network automation lab and how C++ is used in them.

Physical Infrastructure

The physical infrastructure of a network automation lab includes the hardware components that simulate the network. This includes switches, routers, firewalls, servers, and other network devices. The lab infrastructure can be physical or virtual, and it can be set up using commercial software, such as GNS3 or VIRL, or open-source software, such as EVE-NG or OpenStack.

In a physical infrastructure, network devices are connected using cables, while in a virtual infrastructure, network devices are simulated using software. Virtual infrastructure provides more flexibility and scalability as it allows you to create multiple network topologies and switch between them quickly. The choice of infrastructure depends on the lab requirements, the budget, and the availability of resources.

Network Automation Software

Network automation software is a crucial component of a network automation lab, as it provides the automation capabilities required to manage the lab infrastructure. Network automation software can be used to configure, monitor, and troubleshoot the network devices in the lab. It can also be used to automate network tasks, such as provisioning, backup, and software upgrades.

C++ is a programming language that is widely used in network automation software development. C++ is a compiled language that provides low-level control over the hardware, which is essential for network automation. It is also a high-performance language that can handle large amounts of data quickly and efficiently.

Scripting Languages

Scripting languages are used to create automation scripts that automate network tasks.

Automation scripts are typically written in interpreted languages, such as Python, Perl, or Ruby. These languages provide a high-level interface for interacting with network devices, making it easier to write automation scripts.

C++ is not commonly used for scripting as it is a compiled language, and it does not provide the ease of use that scripting languages provide. However, C++ can be used to develop libraries and modules that can be used by scripting languages to perform specific tasks.

Test and Monitoring Tools

Test and monitoring tools are used to test and monitor the lab infrastructure. Test tools are used to verify the functionality of the network devices, while monitoring tools are used to monitor the performance of the network devices and detect any issues.

Test tools can be developed using C++, as it provides low-level control over the hardware and can interact directly with the network devices. Monitoring tools, on the other hand, can be developed using higher-level languages, such as Python or Ruby, which provide a more accessible interface for monitoring the network devices.

Data Analysis and Visualization Tools

Data analysis and visualization tools are used to analyze the data generated by the lab infrastructure and visualize it in a meaningful way. These tools can be used to identify trends, detect anomalies, and make predictions about the behavior of the network.

C++ can be used to develop data analysis and visualization tools, as it provides high-performance capabilities that are required for processing large amounts of data. However, higher-level languages, such as Python or R, are more commonly used for data analysis and visualization due to their ease of use and availability of libraries.

To summarize, a network automation lab is a testing environment that simulates a network, allowing engineers to experiment with different configurations and scenarios. C++ is a programming language that is widely used in network automation labs due to its performance, flexibility, and robustness. The components of a network automation lab include physical infrastructure, network automation software, scripting languages, test and monitoring tools, and data analysis and visualization tools.

Physical infrastructure can be physical or virtual and includes network devices such as switches, routers, firewalls, and servers. Network automation software provides automation capabilities to manage the lab infrastructure, including configuring, monitoring, and troubleshooting network devices. Scripting languages are used to create automation scripts that automate network tasks.

Test and monitoring tools are used to test and monitor the lab infrastructure. Test tools verify the functionality of the network devices, while monitoring tools monitor the performance of the network devices and detect any issues. Data analysis and visualization tools are used to analyze the data generated by the lab infrastructure and visualize it in a meaningful way.

C++ is used in various components of a network automation lab, including network automation software, test tools, and data analysis and visualization tools. C++ provides low-level control over the hardware, making it suitable for interacting directly with network devices. It is also a high-performance language that can handle large amounts of data quickly and efficiently. However, higher-level languages such as Python or Ruby are more commonly used for scripting and data analysis due to their ease of use and availability of libraries.

In summary, a network automation lab with C++ language involves a combination of physical infrastructure, network automation software, scripting languages, test and monitoring tools, and data analysis and visualization tools. The use of C++ in network automation labs provides performance, flexibility, and robustness in various components. However, other programming languages may be better suited for certain tasks, and the choice of language depends on the lab requirements and the availability of resources.

Setting Up GNS3 Network Simulator

GNS3 is a popular open-source network simulator that allows you to simulate and test complex network configurations without the need for physical hardware. It provides a graphical user interface that allows you to drag and drop network devices and configure their properties. GNS3 is available on multiple platforms, including Linux, and supports a wide range of network devices, including routers, switches, and firewalls. In this section, we will discuss how to install GNS3 on Linux and how to support C++ in GNS3.

Install Dependencies

Before installing GNS3, we need to install some dependencies. These dependencies may vary depending on the Linux distribution you are using. In this section, we will be using Ubuntu as an example.

To install the dependencies, open the terminal and type the following command:

```
sudo apt-get update
sudo apt-get install git python3-setuptools python3-pyqt5 python3-pyqt5.qtwebengine python3-ws4py python3-netifaces python3-jsonschema python3-psutil python3-requests python3-aiohttp libvirt-clients libvirt-daemon-system qemu-kvm libguestfs-tools uml-utilities virt-manager wireshark
```

This command will install the necessary packages required for running GNS3.

Install GNS3

To install GNS3 on Linux, we will use pip3, which is a package manager for Python. Open the terminal and type the following command:

```
sudo apt-get install python3-pip
```

Once pip3 is installed, we can use it to install GNS3. Type the following command:

```
sudo pip3 install gns3-gui
```

This command will install the GNS3 graphical user interface.

Install Dynamips

Dynamips is a Cisco router emulator that is used by GNS3 to emulate Cisco IOS images. To install Dynamips, type the following command in the terminal:

```
sudo apt-get install dynamips
```

This command will install Dynamips on your Linux machine.

Install C++ Libraries

To support C++ in GNS3, we need to install the appropriate C++ libraries. In the below sample program, we will be installing the libpcap and libtins libraries.

To install libpcap, type the following command:

```
sudo apt-get install libpcap-dev
```

This command will install the libpcap development libraries.

To install libtins, we need to download the source code and compile it. Type the following commands in the terminal:

```
git clone https://github.com/mfontanini/libtins.git
cd libtins
mkdir build
cd build
cmake ../
make
sudo make install
```

This will download the libtins source code, compile it, and install it on your Linux machine.

Configure GNS3

Once GNS3 is installed, we need to configure it to support C++. Open GNS3 and go to Edit -> Preferences. Click on the General tab and scroll down to the Command line options section. In the Dynamips path field, type the following:

```
./dynamips -P 5000
```

This command will start the Dynamips emulator on port 5000.

Next, go to the Capture tab and select libpcap as the capture method. In the libpcap path field, type the following:

```
/usr/include
```

This will tell GNS3 where to find the libpcap libraries.

Finally, go to the Capture tab and select the Tins capture method. In the Tins path field, type the following:

```
/usr/local/lib
```

This will tell GNS3 where to find the libtins libraries.

Create Network Topology

Once GNS3 is configured, we can create a network topology. Click on the New Blank Project button in the toolbar to create a new project. This will open the GNS3 workspace.

To create a network topology, drag and drop network devices from the Devices panel on the left-hand side of the screen. Configure the properties of the network devices by double-clicking on them.

Configure C++ Support in Network Devices

To support C++ in network devices, we need to configure the appropriate settings in their configuration files. In the below sample program, we will be configuring a Cisco router to support C++.

Double-click on the Cisco router and select the console tab. This will open the console for the router. Type the following commands:

```
enable
configure terminal
interface fastEthernet 0/0
ip address 192.168.1.1 255.255.255.0
no shutdown
exit
```

This will configure the fastEthernet 0/0 interface of the router with an IP address of 192.168.1.1 and enable it.

Next, we need to configure the router to support C++. Type the following commands:

```
configure terminal
```

```
ip tcp path-mtu-discovery
ip tcp selective-ack
ip tcp timestamp
ip tcp window-size 8192
ip tcp synwait-time 5
ip tcp synwait-time 10
ip tcp synwait-time 15
ip tcp synwait-time 20
exit
```

These commands will configure the router to support C++.

Test Network Topologies

Once the network topology is configured, we can test it to ensure that it is functioning correctly. Click on the Start button in the toolbar to start the network devices.

Open a terminal and type the following command to ping the Cisco router:

```
ping 192.168.1.1
```

If the ping is successful, the network topology is functioning correctly.

To summarize, we discussed how to install GNS3 on Linux and how to support C++ in GNS3. We first installed the necessary dependencies and then installed GNS3 using pip3. We then installed Dynamips, libpcap, and libtins to support C++. We configured GNS3 to support C++ by specifying the appropriate paths to the libraries. We created a network topology and configured a Cisco router to support C++. Finally, we tested the network topology to ensure that it was functioning correctly. By following these steps, you can easily install GNS3 on Linux and support C++ in GNS3.

Installing and Configuring C++

To install C++ for a network automation lab, we need to first ensure that we have a C++ compiler installed on our system. In the below sample program, we will be using the g++ compiler on a Linux system.

Install C++ Compiler

To install the g++ compiler on a Debian-based Linux system, open a terminal and type the following command:

```
sudo apt-get update
sudo apt-get install g++
```

This will install the g++ compiler on your system.

Create C++ Program

To create a C++ program, open a text editor and create a new file with a .cpp extension. In the below sample program, we will create a simple program that prints the message "Hello, world!" to the console.

Type the following code into the text editor:

```
#include <iostream>

using namespace std;

int main()
{
   cout << "Hello, world!" << endl;
   return 0;
}
```

Save the file as "hello.cpp" in your home directory.

Compile C++ Program

To compile the C++ program, open a terminal and navigate to the directory where the "hello.cpp" file is saved.

Type the following command to compile the program:

```
g++ hello.cpp -o hello
```

This will compile the program and generate an executable file named "hello".

Run C++ Program

To run the C++ program, type the following command into the terminal:

```
./hello
```

This will execute the program and print the message "Hello, world!" to the console.

Incorporate C++ in Network Automation Lab

Now that we have successfully installed and tested C++, we can incorporate it into our network automation lab.

To do this, we need to create a C++ program that interacts with the network devices in our lab. This program can be used to automate repetitive tasks, gather data, or configure devices.

For example, we could create a program that sends commands to a router and retrieves the output. To do this, we would need to use a library such as libtins to send and receive packets, and the Boost C++ libraries to parse the output.

To use these libraries in our program, we would need to install them on our system. To install libtins, open a terminal and type the following command:

```
sudo apt-get install libtins-dev
```

This will install the libtins library and its development files on your system.

To install the Boost libraries, open a terminal and type the following command:

```
sudo apt-get install libboost-all-dev
```

This will install all the Boost libraries and their development files on your system.

Once these libraries are installed, we can use them in our C++ program to interact with network devices.

Just to conclude, We first installed the g++ compiler on our system and then created a simple C++ program. We compiled and executed the program to ensure that it was functioning correctly. We then discussed how to incorporate C++ into a network automation lab by creating a program that interacts with network devices using libraries such as libtins and the Boost C++ libraries. By following these steps, you can easily install and use C++ in your network automation lab.

Installing Eclipse IDE

To install Eclipse IDE for use in a network automation lab, you can follow these steps:

Download Eclipse IDE

First, navigate to the Eclipse download page at https://www.eclipse.org/downloads/ and download the appropriate version of Eclipse IDE for your operating system.

Install Eclipse IDE

Once the download is complete, extract the Eclipse archive to a directory of your choice. In the below sample program, we will extract it to the "/opt" directory.

Open a terminal and navigate to the directory where you have downloaded the Eclipse archive. Then, type the following command to extract the archive:

```
sudo tar xzf eclipse*.tar.gz -C /opt/
```

This will extract the Eclipse files to the "/opt" directory.

Run Eclipse IDE

To run Eclipse IDE, navigate to the "/opt/eclipse" directory and double-click on the "eclipse" executable file. Alternatively, you can run it from the terminal by typing the following command:

```
/opt/eclipse/eclipse
```

The Eclipse IDE will launch.

Install Required Plugins

To use Eclipse for network automation, we need to install some plugins that provide support for the required programming languages and tools.

The following are some commonly used plugins:

- C/C++ Development Tools (CDT): provides support for C/C++ programming language
- PyDev: provides support for Python programming language
- Eclipse Git Team Provider: provides support for Git version control system
- Eclipse Marketplace Client: allows easy installation of additional plugins

To install these plugins, open Eclipse and navigate to the Help > Eclipse Marketplace menu. In the Eclipse Marketplace window, search for the required plugin and click the Install button.

Create Project

Once you have installed the required plugins, you can create a new project in Eclipse. To do this, navigate to the File > New > C++ Project menu. In the C++ Project window, select the appropriate project type and click the Next button. Follow the prompts to configure the project settings.

Write and Run Code

Now that you have created a project, you can write and run your code. To create a new source file, right-click on the project in the Project Explorer window and select New > Source File. Write your code in the editor and save the file.

To run the code, click the Run button on the toolbar or navigate to the Run > Run menu. The output will be displayed in the Console window.

By following these steps, you can install and use Eclipse IDE for network automation lab. Eclipse provides a powerful and flexible environment for developing, testing, and deploying network automation scripts in various programming languages. With the right plugins and configurations, you can leverage the full power of Eclipse to automate your network operations and improve your network efficiency.

Configure cpp-netlib, Boost, OpenSSL, and zlib

To configure cpp-netlib, Boost, OpenSSL, and zlib for C++ networking, you can follow these steps:

Install Required Libraries

Before configuring cpp-netlib, Boost, OpenSSL, and zlib, you need to ensure that they are installed on your system. To install these libraries, use your system's package manager or download them from their respective websites and follow the installation instructions.

Download cpp-netlib

To download cpp-netlib, navigate to the cpp-netlib GitHub page at https://github.com/cpp-netlib/cpp-netlib and download the latest release.

Extract cpp-netlib

Once the download is complete, extract the cpp-netlib archive to a directory of your choice. In the below sample program, we will extract it to the "/opt" directory.

Open a terminal and navigate to the directory where you have downloaded the cpp-netlib archive. Then, type the following command to extract the archive:

```
sudo tar xzf cpp-netlib*.tar.gz -C /opt/
```

This will extract the cpp-netlib files to the "/opt" directory.

Build cpp-netlib

To build cpp-netlib, navigate to the "/opt/cpp-netlib" directory and run the following commands:

```
./bootstrap.sh
./configure --with-boost-libdir=<BOOST_LIB_DIR> --with-boost-include=<BOOST_INCLUDE_DIR> --with-openssl=<OPENSSL_DIR> --with-zlib=<ZLIB_DIR>
```

```
make
sudo make install
```

Replace the <BOOST_LIB_DIR>, <BOOST_INCLUDE_DIR>, <OPENSSL_DIR>, and <ZLIB_DIR> with the appropriate paths on your system.

Test cpp-netlib

To test cpp-netlib, navigate to the "/opt/cpp-netlib/examples" directory and run the following commands:

```
make
./server &
./client http://localhost:8080
```

This will start a web server on port 8080 and a client that sends a request to the server. If everything is configured correctly, the client should receive a response from the server.

By following these steps, you can configure cpp-netlib, Boost, OpenSSL, and zlib for C++ networking. cpp-netlib provides a powerful and flexible framework for building high-performance network applications using the C++ programming language. With the right configurations, you can leverage the full power of cpp-netlib to develop network applications that meet your specific requirements.

Configuring Ports

Configuring ports with C++ scripting and the installed libraries is an important step in network automation. The following are the steps to configure ports using C++ scripting with the installed libraries:

Import Libraries

The first step is to import the required libraries into your C++ code. For example, to use cpp-netlib for networking, you can add the following code to your header file:

```
#include <boost/network/protocol/http/client.hpp>
#include <boost/network/uri.hpp>
```

```
#include <boost/network/uri/uri_io.hpp>
```

Similarly, if you need to use OpenSSL for secure networking, you can add the following code:

```
#include <openssl/ssl.h>
#include <openssl/err.h>
```

Define Port Number and IP Address

Next, you need to define the port number and IP address of the device you want to configure. For example, to configure the port number and IP address of a device with IP address 192.168.0.1 and port number 8080, you can define the following variables:

```
std::string ip_address = "192.168.0.1";
std::string port = "8080";
```

Open Connection

To establish a connection with the device, you can use the following code:

```
boost::asio::io_service io_service;
boost::asio::ip::tcp::resolver resolver(io_service);
boost::asio::ip::tcp::resolver::query query(ip_address, port);
boost::asio::ip::tcp::socket socket(io_service);
boost::asio::connect(socket, resolver.resolve(query));
```

This code uses the Boost.Asio library to open a TCP socket and connect to the specified IP address and port number.

Send Configuration Commands

Once the connection is established, you can send configuration commands to the device using the socket. For example, to send a command to enable port 1, you can use the following code:

```
std::string command = "enable port 1";
boost::asio::write(socket, boost::asio::buffer(command));
```

Receive Response

After sending the command, you can receive the response from the device using the following code:

```
std::vector<char> response(boost::asio::buffer_size(response_buffer));
boost::asio::read(socket, boost::asio::buffer(response));
```

This code uses a buffer to receive the response from the device. You can then process the response and take appropriate actions based on the results.

Close Connection

Finally, after completing the configuration tasks, you need to close the connection using the following code:

```
socket.shutdown(boost::asio::ip::tcp::socket::shutdown_both);
socket.close();
```

This code uses the Boost.Asio library to shutdown the socket and close the connection with the device.

In summary, configuring ports with C++ scripting and the installed libraries involves importing the required libraries, defining the port number and IP address, opening a connection, sending configuration commands, receiving responses, and closing the connection. By following these steps, you can automate network configuration tasks using C++ and leverage the power of the installed libraries for networking.

Configuring Hosts (Multiple)

Configuring hosts with C++ scripting and the installed libraries is another important aspect of network automation. The following are the steps to configure hosts using C++ scripting with the installed libraries:

Import Libraries

The first step is to import the required libraries into your C++ code. For example, to use cpp-netlib for networking, you can add the following code to your header file:

```
#include <boost/network/protocol/http/client.hpp>
#include <boost/network/uri.hpp>
#include <boost/network/uri/uri_io.hpp>
```

Similarly, if you need to use OpenSSL for secure networking, you can add the following code:

```
#include <openssl/ssl.h>
#include <openssl/err.h>
```

Define Host IP Address

Next, you need to define the IP address of the host you want to configure. For example, to configure the host with IP address 192.168.0.2, you can define the following variable:

```
std::string ip_address = "192.168.0.2";
```

Open Connection

To establish a connection with the host, you can use the following code:

```
boost::asio::io_service io_service;
boost::asio::ip::tcp::endpoint
endpoint(boost::asio::ip::address::from_string(ip_address), 0);
boost::asio::ip::tcp::socket socket(io_service);
socket.connect(endpoint);
```

This code uses the Boost.Asio library to open a TCP socket and connect to the specified IP address.

Send Configuration Commands

Once the connection is established, you can send configuration commands to the host using the socket. For example, to send a command to set the hostname to "myhost", you can use the following code:

```
std::string command = "hostnamectl set-hostname myhost";
boost::asio::write(socket, boost::asio::buffer(command));
```

Receive Response

After sending the command, you can receive the response from the host using the following code:

```
std::vector<char> response(boost::asio::buffer_size(response_buffer));
boost::asio::read(socket, boost::asio::buffer(response));
```

This code uses a buffer to receive the response from the host. You can then process the response and take appropriate actions based on the results.

Close Connection

Finally, after completing the configuration tasks, you need to close the connection using the following code:

```
socket.shutdown(boost::asio::ip::tcp::socket::shutdown_both);
socket.close();
```

This code uses the Boost.Asio library to shutdown the socket and close the connection with the host.

In summary, configuring hosts with C++ scripting and the installed libraries involves importing the required libraries, defining the IP address of the host, opening a connection, sending configuration commands, receiving responses, and closing the connection. By following these steps, you can automate host configuration tasks using C++ and leverage the power of the installed libraries for networking.

Configuring Servers

Configuring servers with C++ scripting and the installed libraries is another important aspect of network automation. The following are the steps to configure servers using C++ scripting with the installed libraries:

Import Libraries

The first step is to import the required libraries into your C++ code. For example, to use Boost.Asio for networking, you can add the following code to your header file:

```
#include <boost/asio.hpp>
```

Similarly, if you need to use OpenSSL for secure networking, you can add the following code:

```
#include <openssl/ssl.h>
#include <openssl/err.h>
```

Define Server IP Address and Port

Next, you need to define the IP address and port of the server you want to configure. For example, to configure the server with IP address 192.168.0.1 and port 80, you can define the following variables:

```
std::string server_address = "192.168.0.1";
unsigned short server_port = 80;
```

Create Server Object

To create a server object, you can use the following code:

```
boost::asio::io_service io_service;
boost::asio::ip::tcp::acceptor acceptor(io_service,
boost::asio::ip::tcp::endpoint(boost::asio::ip::address::from_string(server_addre
ss), server_port));
```

This code creates an acceptor object that listens for incoming connections on the specified IP address and port.

Accept Incoming Connections

To accept incoming connections, you can use the following code:

```
boost::asio::ip::tcp::socket socket(io_service);
acceptor.accept(socket);
```

This code blocks until a connection is established and returns a socket object for the connection.

Receive Configuration Commands

Once a connection is established, you can receive configuration commands from the client using the socket. For example, to receive a command to set the hostname, you can use the following code:

```
boost::asio::streambuf command_buffer;
boost::asio::read_until(socket, command_buffer, "\n");
std::string command(boost::asio::buffers_begin(command_buffer.data()),
boost::asio::buffers_end(command_buffer.data()));
```

This code uses a buffer to receive the command from the client and converts it to a string.

Process Command

After receiving the command, you can process it and take appropriate actions based on the results. For example, to set the hostname to "myhost", you can use the following code:

```
system(("hostnamectl set-hostname " + command).c_str());
```

This code uses the system function to execute the command on the server.

Send Response

After processing the command, you can send a response to the client using the following code:

```
std::string response = "Command executed successfully";
boost::asio::write(socket, boost::asio::buffer(response));
```

This code uses the socket to send the response to the client.

Close Connection

Finally, after completing the configuration tasks, you need to close the connection using the following code:

```
socket.shutdown(boost::asio::ip::tcp::socket::shutdown_both);
socket.close();
```

This code uses the socket to shutdown the connection with the client.

In summary, configuring servers with C++ scripting and the installed libraries involves importing the required libraries, defining the IP address and port of the server, creating a server object, accepting incoming connections, receiving configuration commands, processing commands, sending responses, and closing the connection. By following these steps, you can automate server configuration tasks using C++ and leverage the power of the installed libraries for networking.

Configuring Encryption for Networks

Configuring network encryption with C++ scripting and the installed libraries is an essential step for secure network communication.
The following are the steps to configure network encryption using C++ scripting with the installed libraries:

Import Libraries

The first step is to import the required libraries into your C++ code. For example, to use OpenSSL for secure networking, you can add the following code to your header file:

```
#include <openssl/ssl.h>
#include <openssl/err.h>
```

Initialize OpenSSL

Next, you need to initialize OpenSSL in your code using the following code:

```
SSL_library_init();
SSL_load_error_strings();
OpenSSL_add_all_algorithms();
```

This code initializes the OpenSSL library and loads error strings and algorithms.

Define SSL Context

To configure network encryption, you need to define an SSL context. An SSL context is a configuration that defines how the SSL connection will be established. For example, to configure an SSL context with SSLv23_method and TLSv1.2, you can use the following code:

```
SSL_CTX *ssl_ctx = SSL_CTX_new(SSLv23_method());
SSL_CTX_set_options(ssl_ctx, SSL_OP_NO_SSLv2 | SSL_OP_NO_SSLv3 |
SSL_OP_NO_COMPRESSION);
SSL_CTX_set_min_proto_version(ssl_ctx, TLS1_2_VERSION);
```

This code creates an SSL context object, sets the SSL options to disable SSLv2, SSLv3, and compression, and sets the minimum protocol version to TLSv1.2.

Load SSL Certificates

To establish an SSL connection, you need to load SSL certificates. SSL certificates are used to verify the identity of the server and client. For example, to load the server certificate and key from a file, you can use the following code:

```
SSL_CTX_use_certificate_file(ssl_ctx, "server.crt", SSL_FILETYPE_PEM);
SSL_CTX_use_PrivateKey_file(ssl_ctx, "server.key", SSL_FILETYPE_PEM);
```

This code loads the server certificate and key from the PEM file.

Create SSL Socket

To create an SSL socket, you can use the following code:

```
int server_socket = socket(AF_INET, SOCK_STREAM, IPPROTO_TCP);
SSL *ssl = SSL_new(ssl_ctx);
SSL_set_fd(ssl, server_socket);
```

This code creates a TCP socket and an SSL object, associates the SSL object with the socket, and sets the SSL options.

Accept SSL Connection

To accept an SSL connection, you can use the following code:

```
struct sockaddr_in server_address;
socklen_t server_address_len = sizeof(server_address);
int client_socket = accept(server_socket, (struct sockaddr *)&server_address,
&server_address_len);
SSL_set_accept_state(ssl);
SSL_set_fd(ssl, client_socket);
SSL_accept(ssl);
```

This code accepts a connection on the server socket, sets the SSL object to the accept state, associates the SSL object with the client socket, and performs the SSL handshake.

Receive Encrypted Data

Once the SSL connection is established, you can receive encrypted data from the client using the SSL socket. For example, to receive encrypted data from the client, you can use the following code:

```
char buffer[1024];
int bytes_received = SSL_read(ssl, buffer, sizeof(buffer));
```

This code reads encrypted data from the SSL socket and returns the number of bytes received.

Decrypt Data

After receiving encrypted data, you need to decrypt it using the SSL socket. For example, to decrypt the received data, you can use the following code:

```
std::string decrypted_data;
char buffer[1024];
int bytes_received = SSL_read(ssl, buffer, sizeof(buffer));
decrypted_data = std::string(buffer, bytes_received);
```

This code creates a string object to store the decrypted data, reads encrypted data from the SSL socket into a buffer, and decrypts the data using the SSL object.

Send Encrypted Data

After decrypting the data, you can process it and send a response back to the client. To send encrypted data, you can use the following code:

```
std::string response = "Response data";
int bytes_sent = SSL_write(ssl, response.c_str(), response.length());
```

This code creates a response string, sends the response to the client using the SSL socket, and returns the number of bytes sent.

Close SSL Connection

To close the SSL connection, you can use the following code:

```
SSL_shutdown(ssl);
close(client_socket);
```

This code performs an SSL shutdown and closes the client socket.

To summarize, configuring network encryption with C++ scripting and the installed libraries is a crucial step in ensuring secure network communication. By importing the required libraries, initializing OpenSSL, defining an SSL context, loading SSL certificates, creating an SSL socket, accepting an SSL connection, receiving encrypted data, decrypting data, sending encrypted data, and closing the SSL connection, you can ensure that your network communication is secure and protected against potential security threats.

Testing Complete Automation Setup

Testing a network automation lab is an essential step to ensure that all the components are working correctly and that the network is set up as intended. There are several ways to test a network automation lab, including testing the simulator, installed libraries, ports, hosts, and servers.

Testing Simulator

The first step in testing the network automation lab is to test the simulator. To test the simulator, you can create a simple network topology using the simulator and test the network's connectivity. You can create different network topologies, including star topology, ring topology, and mesh topology, to test the network's scalability.

To test the network connectivity, you can ping different hosts in the network and verify that they are reachable. You can also test the bandwidth and latency of the network by transferring data between different hosts in the network. Additionally, you can use network monitoring tools like Wireshark to capture and analyze network traffic and identify any network issues.

Testing Installed Libraries

The next step is to test the installed libraries to ensure that they are working correctly. To test the installed libraries, you can write sample programs that use the libraries and test their functionality. For example, if you have installed Boost, you can write a C++ program that uses Boost libraries to perform various networking operations, such as sending and receiving data over the network, creating sockets, and handling network errors.

Similarly, you can write a sample program that uses OpenSSL libraries to encrypt and decrypt data over the network. You can also test the zlib library by compressing and decompressing data using the library's functions.

Testing Ports

To test the ports, you can create a simple server-client application that listens on a specific port and sends data to the server. You can use the netcat utility to test the ports. For example, to test port 80, you can run the following command:

```
$ nc -vz <server_ip> 80
```

This command sends a TCP SYN packet to the server's port 80 and waits for a response. If the port is open, the server responds with a TCP SYN/ACK packet, and the netcat utility prints a success message. Otherwise, it prints a failure message.

Similarly, you can test other ports in the network and ensure that they are functioning correctly.

Testing Hosts

To test the hosts, you can perform various network operations, such as sending and receiving data, creating sockets, and handling network errors. You can write sample programs in C++ that perform these operations and test their functionality.

Additionally, you can test the hosts' security by performing various security tests, such as port scanning, vulnerability testing, and penetration testing. You can use security testing tools like Nmap, Metasploit, and Burp Suite to perform these tests and identify any security issues in the network.

Testing Servers

To test the servers, you can create different server-client applications that perform various network operations, such as sending and receiving data, creating sockets, and handling network errors. You can test the servers' scalability by creating multiple server instances and load-balancing the traffic between them.

Additionally, you can test the servers' security by performing various security tests, such as penetration testing, vulnerability testing, and intrusion detection. You can use security testing tools like Nmap, Metasploit, and Burp Suite to perform these tests and identify any security issues in the network.

Overall, testing a network automation lab is an essential step in ensuring that the network is set up as intended and is functioning correctly. By testing the simulator, installed libraries, ports, hosts, and servers, you can identify any issues in the network and address them promptly. Additionally, testing the network's security is crucial to ensure that the network is

Summary

In this chapter, we discussed the concept of a network automation lab, which is a testing environment used for developing and testing network automation solutions. We went through the different components of a network automation lab, including the network simulator, C++ programming language, GNS3, Eclipse IDE, cpp-netlib, Boost, OpenSSL, and zlib libraries. We also discussed how to configure the ports, hosts, and servers using C++ scripting and the installed libraries.

To test the network automation lab, we discussed different testing methods for the simulator, installed libraries, ports, hosts, and servers. For the simulator, we recommended creating a simple network topology and testing network connectivity by pinging different hosts and testing bandwidth and latency. For the installed libraries, we suggested writing sample programs that use the libraries and testing their functionality, including testing OpenSSL libraries for encryption and decryption and testing the zlib library for compression and decompression. We also discussed how to test the ports using the netcat utility, test hosts using C++ programming, and test servers using different server-client applications.

Finally, we emphasized the importance of testing the network's security using various security testing tools like Nmap, Metasploit, and Burp Suite. We recommended performing different security tests such as penetration testing, vulnerability testing, and intrusion detection to identify any security issues in the network and address them promptly.

In summary, setting up a network automation lab requires configuring different components such as the simulator, programming language, libraries, ports, hosts, and servers. Testing the network automation lab is crucial to ensure that the network is set up as intended and functioning correctly. Different testing methods like network connectivity, sample programming, netcat utility, server-client applications, and security testing tools can be used to test the network automation lab. By following the steps outlined in this chapter, one can set up and test a network automation lab for various networking operations.

CHAPTER 4: SCRIPT, TEST, AND VALIDATE NETWORK AUTOMATION

Understanding Network Automation Scripts

Overview

Network automation scripts are essential tools that help network engineers automate various network management and operation tasks. These scripts are written in various programming languages, including C++. C++ is a high-performance language that offers features like low-level memory manipulation and multithreading, making it a popular choice for network automation scripting.

The concept of network automation scripts using C++ involves creating programs that interact with the network using the C++ programming language. These scripts can automate various tasks like configuration management, network monitoring, and network troubleshooting, among others. The following are some of the key concepts involved in writing network automation scripts using C++.

Networking APIs and Libraries

Network automation scripts rely on various libraries and APIs to interact with the network. C++ provides several networking libraries and APIs, including the Boost C++ Libraries, cpp-netlib, and OpenSSL, among others. These libraries and APIs provide network functionality like socket programming, SSL encryption, HTTP/HTTPS protocols, and many others, making them an essential part of network automation scripting.

Data Structures and Algorithms

Data structures and algorithms are critical in network automation scripting, as they help in manipulating data and performing various network operations. C++ offers a wide range of data structures, including arrays, lists, queues, and maps, among others. Algorithms like searching, sorting, and graph traversal algorithms are also essential in network automation scripting.

Object-Oriented Programming

C++ is an object-oriented language, and network automation scripts can take advantage of its features like encapsulation, inheritance, and polymorphism. Using object-oriented programming, network automation scripts can create objects that represent different network entities like routers, switches, and hosts, among others. These objects can be manipulated to perform various network operations.

Multithreading

Multithreading is a feature that allows programs to execute multiple threads concurrently, making it a crucial concept in network automation scripting. Using multithreading, network automation scripts can perform multiple tasks concurrently, enhancing the efficiency and speed of network operations.

Error Handling

Error handling is an essential concept in network automation scripting, as it helps in detecting and handling errors that may arise during network operations. C++ provides various error handling mechanisms like exceptions and error codes, which can be used to detect and handle errors in network automation scripts.

Hence, network automation scripts using C++ are an essential tool for network engineers, as they help in automating various network management and operation tasks. The concepts involved in writing network automation scripts using C++ include networking libraries and APIs, data structures and algorithms, object-oriented programming, multithreading, and error handling, among others. By leveraging these concepts, network automation scripts can be written to perform different network operations effectively and efficiently.

C++ Network Automation Scripting Process

Writing network automation scripts in C++ involves the following steps:

Define Objective

The first step in writing network automation scripts is to define the objective of the script. This involves identifying the network operation that needs to be automated and outlining the requirements and specifications of the script.

Plan and Design Script

The next step is to plan and design the script. This involves breaking down the objective into smaller tasks and designing a flowchart or algorithm that outlines the steps that the script will take to achieve the objective.

Choose Libraries and APIs

Once the script's design is complete, the next step is to choose the libraries and APIs that will be used to interact with the network. C++ provides several networking libraries and

APIs like Boost C++ Libraries, cpp-netlib, and OpenSSL, among others. Choosing the appropriate libraries and APIs is critical to the success of the script.

Write Script

The next step is to write the script. This involves writing the code in C++ that implements the algorithm or flowchart designed in step two. The script should be written with readability and maintainability in mind, as it may need to be updated or modified in the future.

Test Script

Once the script is written, the next step is to test it. This involves running the script in a test environment and verifying that it performs the intended operation correctly. Testing should include various scenarios to ensure that the script is robust and can handle different network conditions and environments.

Validate Script

After testing, the next step is to validate the script. This involves verifying that the script meets the requirements and specifications defined in step one. Validation may involve testing the script in a production environment or running it through various validation processes.

Document Script

The final step is to document the script. This involves creating documentation that outlines the script's purpose, design, libraries and APIs used, and how to run and maintain the script. Proper documentation is critical in ensuring that the script can be maintained and updated effectively.

Overall, writing network automation scripts in C++ involves defining the objective, planning and designing the script, choosing the appropriate libraries and APIs, writing the code, testing and validating the script, and documenting the script. By following these steps, network engineers can create effective and efficient scripts that can automate various network operations.

Define C++ Variables for Automation

To define variables for automation scripts in C++, you need to follow the steps below:

Open C++ IDE

First, you need to open an Integrated Development Environment (IDE) for C++ such as Eclipse, Visual Studio Code, or Code::Blocks.

Create New C++ Project

Create a new C++ project in the IDE and name it according to your preference.

Define Variables

To define a variable in C++, you need to specify its data type and identifier. For example, to define an integer variable named "myInteger", you would write:

```
int myInteger;
```

Similarly, to define a string variable named "myString", you would write:

```
td::string myString;
```

Assign Values to Variables

To assign a value to a variable, you need to use the assignment operator "=". For example, to assign the value 10 to the integer variable "myInteger", you would write:

```
myInteger = 10;
```

Similarly, to assign the value "hello" to the string variable "myString", you would write:

```
myString = "hello";
```

Alternatively, you can also initialize the variable when it is defined, like this:

```
int myInteger = 10;
std::string myString = "hello";
```

Use Variables in Script

After defining and assigning values to the variables, you can use them in your script. For example, to print the value of the integer variable "myInteger" to the console, you would write:

```
std::cout << "The value of myInteger is: " << myInteger << std::endl;
```

Similarly, to concatenate the string variable "myString" with another string and print it to the console, you would write:

```
std::string anotherString = " world!";
std::cout << myString + anotherString << std::endl;
```

Run Script

Finally, you can run the script and see the output in the console. The output of the above example scripts would be:

```
The value of myInteger is: 10
hello world!
```

Hence, defining variables for automation scripts in C++ involves specifying their data type and identifier, assigning values to them, and using them in the script. By following the above steps, you can define variables in C++ and use them in your automation scripts.

Writing C++ Automation Scripts

To write a C++ code that performs network automation tasks using library functions and tools, you need to follow the steps below:

Include Necessary Libraries

To use library functions and tools in your code, you need to include the corresponding headers at the beginning of your code. For example, to use the Boost.Asio library for network programming, you need to include the "boost/asio.hpp" header like this:

```
#include <boost/asio.hpp>
```

Define Variables and Objects

Next, you need to define variables and objects that will be used in the automation tasks. For example, to create a TCP socket object for network communication, you can define it like this:

```
boost::asio::io_context io_context;
boost::asio::ip::tcp::socket socket(io_context);
Configure the network settings:
```

Before performing any network automation tasks, you need to configure the network settings such as IP addresses, ports, and protocols. For example, to connect to a server with IP address "192.168.1.100" on port "8080" using TCP protocol, you can configure it like this:

```
boost::asio::ip::tcp::resolver resolver(io_context);
boost::asio::ip::tcp::resolver::results_type endpoints =
   resolver.resolve("192.168.1.100", "8080");
```

Perform Network Automation Tasks

After configuring the network settings, you can perform the necessary automation tasks using the library functions and tools. For example, to connect to the server, you can use the "connect" function like this:

```
boost::asio::connect(socket, endpoints);
```

Similarly, to send a message to the server, you can use the "write_some" function like this:

```
std::string message = "Hello server!";
boost::asio::write_some(socket, boost::asio::buffer(message));
```

And to receive a message from the server, you can use the "read_some" function like this:

```
char buffer[1024];
size_t len = socket.read_some(boost::asio::buffer(buffer, 1024));
std::cout << "Received message from server: " << std::string(buffer, len) <<
std::endl;
```

Handle Errors and Exceptions

During the network automation tasks, there might be errors or exceptions that need to be handled properly. For example, if the connection to the server fails, you can handle it like this:

```
try {
  boost::asio::connect(socket, endpoints);
} catch (boost::system::system_error& e) {
  std::cerr << "Connection error: " << e.what() << std::endl;
}
```

Close Network Connection

Finally, after the automation tasks are completed, you need to close the network connection. For example, you can close the socket object like this:

```
socket.close();
```

Hence, writing a C++ code that performs network automation tasks using library functions and tools involves including the necessary libraries, defining variables and objects, configuring the network settings, performing the tasks, handling errors and exceptions, and closing the network connection. By following the above steps and using the appropriate library functions and tools, you can write a C++ code that performs the necessary network automation tasks.

Testing C++ Scripts in Test Environment

Testing the network automation C++ code is an essential step to ensure that the code is working as expected before deploying it in a production environment. In this section, we will discuss the steps involved in testing the network automation C++ code by running it on a test environment.

Set Up a Test Environment

Before testing the network automation C++ code, it is essential to set up a test environment that closely mimics the production environment. This will help in identifying and resolving any issues before deploying the code in the production environment. The test environment should have similar hardware, software, and network configurations as the production environment.

Compile C++ Code

Once the test environment is set up, the next step is to compile the C++ code using a C++ compiler. The code should be compiled with the necessary libraries, tools, and flags that were used during development.

Execute C++ Code

After compiling the code, the next step is to execute the C++ code on the test environment. The code should be executed with the necessary parameters and input data to test its functionality. The output generated by the code should be compared with the expected output to ensure that the code is working as expected.

Debugging

If the code does not produce the expected output, the next step is to debug the code to identify the root cause of the issue. Debugging tools such as GDB can be used to step through the code and identify any errors or issues.

Test Edge Cases

Apart from testing the C++ code with regular input data, it is also important to test the code with edge cases such as invalid input, boundary conditions, and error scenarios. This will help in identifying any issues that may arise when the code is deployed in the production environment.

Integration Testing

Once the C++ code has been tested in isolation, the next step is to perform integration testing to ensure that the code works seamlessly with other components of the network infrastructure. Integration testing involves testing the C++ code with other network automation scripts, tools, and devices to ensure that they work together without any issues.

Validation Testing

The final step in testing the network automation C++ code is validation testing. Validation testing involves testing the code in a production-like environment to ensure that it meets the necessary performance, reliability, and security requirements.

In summary, testing the network automation C++ code involves setting up a test environment, compiling the code, executing the code, debugging any issues, testing edge cases, performing integration testing, and validation testing. Following these steps will help in identifying and resolving any issues with the code before deploying it in the production environment.

Debugging Errors and Issues

Debugging is a critical step in the development and testing process of any software application, including network automation scripts written in C++. Debugging allows developers to identify and resolve any errors or issues that may arise during testing. In this section, we will discuss the steps involved in debugging any errors or issues that arise during testing using C++.

Reproduce Error

The first step in debugging any error or issue is to reproduce the error. This involves running the C++ code that is causing the error with the same input data and parameters that caused the error. This will help in replicating the error and identifying its root cause.

Use Debugging Tools

Once the error has been reproduced, the next step is to use debugging tools such as GDB (GNU Debugger) to identify the root cause of the error. GDB is a powerful debugging tool that allows developers to step through the code line by line, set breakpoints, and examine the program's memory and variables.

Analyze Error Messages

When an error occurs, the C++ compiler or runtime environment may produce an error message that provides valuable information about the error. Analyzing the error message can help in identifying the root cause of the error.

Use Print Statements

Another useful debugging technique is to use print statements to print the values of variables and other program data at different stages of the program's execution. This can help in identifying the value of a variable that is causing the error or the point in the program where the error occurred.

Modify Code

Once the root cause of the error has been identified, the next step is to modify the C++ code to fix the error. This may involve changing the code's logic or fixing a syntax error.

Test Modified Code

After modifying the code, the next step is to test the modified code to ensure that the error has been fixed. The code should be tested with the same input data and parameters that caused the error to ensure that the error has been fixed.

Repeat Process

If the error has not been fixed, the debugging process may need to be repeated. This involves going back to step 1 and repeating the process until the error has been identified and fixed.

In summary, debugging any errors or issues that arise during testing using C++ involves reproducing the error, using debugging tools, analyzing error messages, using print statements, modifying the code, testing the modified code, and repeating the process if necessary. Following these steps will help in identifying and resolving any errors or issues that may arise during testing.

Validating Automation Scripts in Production

Validating network automation C++ code on a production environment or devices is an essential step in ensuring that the code is working as intended and will not cause any issues or disruptions when deployed. In this section, we will discuss the steps involved in validating network automation C++ code on a production environment or devices.

Develop Validation Plan

The first step in validating network automation C++ code is to develop a validation plan. The plan should include the validation criteria, test cases, and expected results.

Create Test Environment

The next step is to create a test environment that simulates the production environment.

This involves configuring the test environment with the same network devices, operating systems, and applications as the production environment.

Run Validation Test Cases

Once the test environment has been created, the next step is to run the validation test cases. These test cases should cover all the critical functions and features of the network automation C++ code.

Monitor and Analyze Results

During the validation test, it is essential to monitor and analyze the results to ensure that the code is working as intended. This may involve monitoring the network traffic, examining log files, and analyzing system performance.

Troubleshoot any Issues

If any issues or errors arise during the validation test, the next step is to troubleshoot the issue. This may involve debugging the C++ code, reconfiguring network devices, or modifying the test environment.

Document Validation Results

Once the validation test is complete, it is essential to document the validation results. This includes recording the test results, documenting any issues or errors that were encountered, and documenting any modifications that were made to the test environment or C++ code.

Deploy C++ Code

Once the network automation C++ code has been validated, it can be deployed to the production environment. However, it is essential to ensure that the production environment is properly configured and that the deployment process is carefully planned and executed.

In summary, validating network automation C++ code on a production environment or devices involves developing a validation plan, creating a test environment, running validation test cases, monitoring and analyzing the results, troubleshooting any issues, documenting the validation results, and deploying the C++ code. Following these steps will help ensure that the network automation C++ code is working as intended and will not cause any issues or disruptions when deployed.

Summary

In this chapter, we have discussed in detail the steps involved in writing, testing, and validating network automation scripts using C++.

Firstly, we discussed the conceptual understanding of network automation scripts and the importance of using C++ for network automation. We then moved on to discussing the steps involved in writing, testing, and validating network automation scripts in C++.

We started by describing the process of defining variables for automation scripts in C++. This involved identifying the variables required for network automation tasks, defining their data types, and initializing them with appropriate values.

Next, we discussed how to write the C++ code that performs the necessary network automation tasks using the library functions and tools. This involved understanding the requirements of the network automation task, selecting appropriate library functions and tools, and writing the code to automate the task.

We then moved on to testing the network automation C++ code by running it on a test environment or test devices. We described the steps involved in setting up a test environment, creating test cases, running the test cases, and analyzing the results to ensure that the code is working as expected.

In the next step, we discussed how to debug any errors or issues that arise during testing using C++. We explained the process of identifying the cause of the error, using debugging tools and techniques to isolate and fix the issue, and verifying that the fix has resolved the issue.

Finally, we discussed the process of validating network automation C++ code by running it on the production environment or devices. This involved developing a validation plan, creating a test environment that simulates the production environment, running the validation test cases, monitoring and analyzing the results, troubleshooting any issues, documenting the validation results, and deploying the C++ code.

In summary, writing, testing, and validating network automation scripts in C++ requires a systematic and well-defined approach. It is important to understand the requirements of the network automation task, select appropriate library functions and tools, and write the code to automate the task. Testing and validation are critical steps that ensure the code is working as intended and will not cause any issues or disruptions when deployed. Debugging any issues that arise during testing is also important to ensure that the code is free from errors. By following these steps, network automation scripts can be developed and validated with confidence, leading to efficient and error-free network automation.

CHAPTER 5: AUTOMATING CONFIGURATION MANAGEMENT

Understanding Configuration Management

Overview

Configuration management for networking refers to the process of managing and controlling the changes made to network devices and systems. It involves managing the configurations of devices, such as routers, switches, firewalls, and servers, to ensure that they are secure, reliable, and optimized for performance.

Configuration management is critical for networking because it helps to ensure that devices are properly configured, maintain consistency across devices, and minimize errors and downtime. Proper configuration management can help to avoid security breaches, network outages, and other problems that can impact business operations.

Benefits of Managing Configurations

There are several benefits to implementing configuration management for networking. One of the primary benefits is that it helps to maintain the stability and reliability of the network. By managing the configurations of devices, network administrators can ensure that devices are properly configured and optimized for performance. This can help to reduce network downtime and prevent performance issues.

Another benefit of configuration management is that it can help to improve network security. By managing configurations, network administrators can ensure that devices are properly secured and that security policies are being followed. This can help to prevent security breaches and other security issues that can impact the network.

Configuration management can also help to improve the efficiency of network operations. By managing configurations, network administrators can ensure that devices are consistent and that changes are made in a controlled and consistent manner. This can help to reduce errors and simplify the process of managing the network.

Automation of configuration management using C++ can bring even more benefits to the network. C++ is a powerful programming language that can be used to develop automation scripts that can automate many of the configuration management tasks. By automating these tasks, network administrators can save time and improve efficiency.

One of the primary benefits of automating configuration management with C++ is that it can help to reduce errors and improve consistency. Automation scripts can be developed to ensure that devices are properly configured and that changes are made in a controlled and consistent manner. This can help to reduce errors and ensure that devices are properly configured.

Another benefit of automating configuration management with C++ is that it can help to improve the speed of configuration changes. Automation scripts can be developed to make changes to devices quickly and efficiently, without the need for manual intervention. This can help to reduce the time required to make changes to the network, improving network agility and responsiveness.

Automation of configuration management using C++ can also help to improve network security. By automating security-related tasks, such as applying security policies and updating security configurations, network administrators can ensure that security is properly maintained and that security policies are being followed.

In addition to these benefits, automation of configuration management using C++ can also help to improve scalability and reduce costs. By automating configuration management tasks, network administrators can manage larger networks with fewer resources, reducing costs and improving efficiency.

In summary, configuration management for networking is critical for ensuring the stability, reliability, and security of the network. Automation of configuration management using C++ can bring many benefits, including improved consistency, faster configuration changes, improved security, and reduced costs. By leveraging the power of C++ and automation, network administrators can optimize their network operations and ensure that their networks are secure, reliable, and efficient.

New Server Provisioning with Ansible

Server provisioning is the process of setting up and configuring a new server or virtual machine (VM) for use. This includes installing the operating system, setting up security and access controls, installing software and services, configuring network settings, and ensuring that the server meets the requirements of the application or workload it will be hosting.

In order to provision a server, you will need to use a provisioning tool or framework. C++ does not have built-in support for server provisioning, but there are many tools and libraries available that can be used to automate the process. Following is a sample demonstration of how to use some of these tools to provision a server:

Install Ansible

Ansible is a popular provisioning tool that uses a YAML-based configuration language. To install Ansible on a Linux server, run the following commands:

```
sudo apt-get update
sudo apt-get install ansible
```

Create An Inventory File

An inventory file is used by Ansible to keep track of the servers you want to provision. Create a file called hosts.ini with the following contents:

```
[webservers]
myserver ansible_host=192.168.1.10 ansible_user=myuser
ansible_ssh_private_key_file=/path/to/private/key
```

This inventory file defines a group of servers called "webservers" and specifies the IP address, username, and private key file for a server with the hostname "myserver".

Create Playbook

A playbook is a YAML file that defines the tasks you want to run on the target server(s). Following is an example playbook called setup-server.yml:

```
---
- hosts: webservers
  become: true
  tasks:
    - name: Update apt cache
      apt:
        update_cache: yes

    - name: Install Apache
      apt:
        name: apache2
        state: present

    - name: Start Apache
```

```
  service:
    name: apache2
    state: started
    enabled: true
```

This playbook defines a series of tasks to run on the "webservers" group of servers. It updates the apt cache, installs the Apache web server package, and starts the Apache service.

Run Playbook

To run the playbook, use the following command:

```
ansible-playbook -i hosts.ini setup-server.yml
```

This will run the setup-server.yml playbook on the server specified in the hosts.ini file.

Verify Results

Once the playbook has finished running, you can verify that the server has been provisioned correctly. In the above sample program, you can open a web browser and navigate to the IP address of the server (192.168.1.10) to see the default Apache web page.

Server provisioning is an important aspect of configuration management for networking. By automating the process of setting up and configuring servers, you can ensure that your servers are consistent and reliable, and reduce the risk of human error. C++ may not be the best language for server provisioning tasks, but there are many tools and libraries available that can be used to automate the process. Ansible is just one example of a provisioning tool that can be used with C++ to automate server setup and configuration.

Automate System Settings

Automating system settings with C++ can help streamline the configuration process and save time for network administrators. Given below is a sample demonstration on how to automate system settings using C++:

Define System Settings to Automate

The first step is to identify the system settings that need to be automated. This can include settings related to network connectivity, security, user permissions, and other configuration options.

Import Necessary Libraries

To automate system settings using C++, you will need to import the necessary libraries. This can include libraries for working with the Windows registry, accessing system settings, and other system-related tasks.

Define Variables

Next, define the variables that will be used in the automation script. This can include variables for storing system settings values, user permissions, and other configuration options.

Write Automation Code

With the variables defined, it's time to write the automation code. This will typically involve a series of if/else statements or switch cases that check the current system settings and make changes as needed.

For example, the following C++ code can be used to automate the setting of a Windows registry key:

```
#include <iostream>
#include <Windows.h>

int main()
{
 HKEY hKey;
 LPCSTR                                  lpSubKey                                  =
"SOFTWARE\\Microsoft\\Windows\\CurrentVersion\\Run";
 LPCTSTR lpValueName = "MyApplication";
 LPCSTR lpData = "C:\\MyApplication.exe";

 // Open the registry key
 if      (RegOpenKeyEx(HKEY_LOCAL_MACHINE,       lpSubKey,       0,
```

```
KEY_ALL_ACCESS, &hKey) == ERROR_SUCCESS)
 {
  // Set the registry value
  if (RegSetValueEx(hKey, lpValueName, 0, REG_SZ, (LPBYTE)lpData,
strlen(lpData) + 1) == ERROR_SUCCESS)
  {
   std::cout << "Registry key set successfully" << std::endl;
  }
  else
  {
   std::cout << "Error setting registry key" << std::endl;
  }

  // Close the registry key
  RegCloseKey(hKey);
 }
 else
 {
  std::cout << "Error opening registry key" << std::endl;
 }

 return 0;
}
```

In the above sample program, the code opens the Windows registry key for the "Run" section, sets the value for the "MyApplication" key to "C:\MyApplication.exe", and then closes the key. This would ensure that the specified application is launched automatically when the system boots up.

Test and Validate Automation Code

Once the automation code has been written, it's important to test and validate it on a test system to ensure that it works as expected. This may involve running the code in a sandbox environment or on a virtual machine to avoid affecting production systems.

Deploy Automation Code

Once the code has been tested and validated, it can be deployed to production systems to automate the system settings configuration process. This can help ensure that all systems are configured consistently and according to best practices, and can save time and effort for network administrators.

Overall, automating system settings using C++ can help streamline the configuration process, improve consistency, and save time and effort for network administrators. By following these steps and best practices, you can develop robust and reliable automation scripts that help keep your network running smoothly.

Modify Base Configurations with C++

Base configurations refer to the initial configurations that are required to set up a device or system before it can be used for any specific purpose. These configurations may include setting up network interfaces, configuring IP addresses, enabling required services, and more.

Modifying base configurations using C++ involves writing scripts that can automate the configuration process. Following is a sample demonstration of how to modify base configurations using C++:

Include Necessary Headers

```
#include <iostream>
#include <fstream>
#include <string>
#include <cstdlib>
#include <cstdio>
```

Define Configuration Files

```
// Define the path of the configuration files
#define INTERFACE_CONF_PATH "/etc/network/interfaces"
#define DNS_CONF_PATH "/etc/resolv.conf"
```

Open Configuration Files for Editing

```
// Open the interface configuration file for editing
std::ofstream interface_conf_file;
interface_conf_file.open(INTERFACE_CONF_PATH, std::ios_base::app);
if (!interface_conf_file.is_open()) {
    std::cerr << "Failed to open interface configuration file\n";
    exit(EXIT_FAILURE);
}

// Open the DNS configuration file for editing
std::ofstream dns_conf_file;
dns_conf_file.open(DNS_CONF_PATH, std::ios_base::app);
if (!dns_conf_file.is_open()) {
    std::cerr << "Failed to open DNS configuration file\n";
    exit(EXIT_FAILURE);
}
```

Write New Configurations to Files

```
// Write the new interface configuration
interface_conf_file << "\nauto eth0\niface eth0 inet static\naddress 192.168.1.10\nnetmask 255.255.255.0\ngateway 192.168.1.1\n";

// Write the new DNS configuration
dns_conf_file << "\nnameserver 8.8.8.8\nnameserver 8.8.4.4\n";
Step 5: Close the configuration files

cpp
Copy code
// Close the interface configuration file
```

```
interface_conf_file.close();

// Close the DNS configuration file
dns_conf_file.close();
```

This is a simple example of how to modify base configurations using C++.

However, for more complex configuration management tasks, tools like Ansible can be used.

Modify Base Configurations With Ansible

Following is a sample demonstration of how to use Ansible to modify base configurations:

Install Ansible on Control Machine

```
sudo apt-get update
sudo apt-get install ansible
```

Create Ansible Playbook to Modify Configurations

```
---
- hosts: all
  become: true
  tasks:
    - name: Update interface configuration
      lineinfile:
        path: /etc/network/interfaces
        line: "auto eth0\niface eth0 inet static\naddress
192.168.1.10\nnetmask 255.255.255.0\ngateway 192.168.1.1"
    - name: Update DNS configuration
      lineinfile:
        path: /etc/resolv.conf
```

```
  line: "nameserver 8.8.8.8\nnameserver 8.8.4.4"
```

Run Ansible Playbook on Target Machine(S)

```
ansible-playbook playbook.yml
```

In the above sample program, the lineinfile module of Ansible is used to modify the configuration files on the target machine(s). The become parameter is used to elevate the privilege level to perform the modifications as a privileged user.

Test Base Configurations with Google Test

Overall, automating system settings using C++ can be a powerful tool for configuration management tasks. After modifying the base configurations, it's important to test them to ensure they work as expected. This can be done by running automated tests, such as network tests, system tests, and integration tests. These tests can be written in C++ using testing frameworks like Google Test or Catch2.

For example, let's say we modified the firewall rules on a server to allow incoming traffic on a specific port. We can write a test in C++ to verify that the firewall rule is working properly. Following is an example using Google Test:

```
#include <gtest/gtest.h>
#include <sys/socket.h>
#include <netinet/in.h>
#include <arpa/inet.h>

TEST(FirewallTest, PortOpen) {
  int sock = socket(AF_INET, SOCK_STREAM, 0);
  ASSERT_NE(-1, sock);

  struct sockaddr_in addr;
  memset(&addr, 0, sizeof(addr));
  addr.sin_family = AF_INET;
```

```
  addr.sin_addr.s_addr = inet_addr("127.0.0.1");
  addr.sin_port = htons(8080);

  int rc = connect(sock, (struct sockaddr*)&addr, sizeof(addr));
  EXPECT_EQ(0, rc);

  close(sock);
}
```

This test creates a socket and attempts to connect to port 8080 on localhost. If the connection is successful, the test passes. Otherwise, it fails.

Once we have written our tests, we can automate them using a continuous integration (CI) system like Jenkins or Travis CI. This allows us to run our tests automatically every time we make changes to our configurations, ensuring that our systems are always in a known state.

In addition to testing, it's also important to version control our configurations using a tool like Git. This allows us to track changes to our configurations over time, roll back to previous versions if necessary, and collaborate with others on our configurations.

Overall, automating system settings with C++ can help streamline the process of managing configurations and ensure that our systems are always in a known state. By writing tests and using version control, we can validate our changes and ensure that they are working as expected.

Automate System Identification

System identification is an important task in the configuration management of networking. It involves identifying the system specifications such as the operating system, processor, memory, disk space, etc. In this section, we will explain how to automate system identification using a combination of C++ and Ansible.

First, let's see how to write a C++ program to identify the system specifications. We can use the system() function in C++ to run the command-line utilities that provide the system information.

Identify Systems using C++

Following is an example code that uses C++ to identify the operating system:

```
#include <iostream>
#include <stdio.h>
#include <stdlib.h>

using namespace std;

int main() {
  #ifdef __linux__
    system("echo $(lsb_release -sd)");
  #elif __APPLE__
    system("echo $(sw_vers -productName) $(sw_vers -productVersion)");
  #elif _WIN32
    system("echo %OS%");
  #endif

  return 0;
}
```

In this code, we have used the preprocessor directives to detect the operating system and run the appropriate command-line utility to identify the operating system. For Linux, we have used the lsb_release utility, for macOS, we have used the sw_vers utility, and for Windows, we have used the %OS% environment variable.

We can similarly use other command-line utilities to identify other system specifications such as the processor, memory, and disk space.

Once we have written the C++ program to identify the system specifications, we can use Ansible to automate the system identification process across multiple devices.

Identify Systems using Ansible

Following is an example playbook that uses the command module of Ansible to run the

C++ program on multiple devices:

```
---
- hosts: all
  gather_facts: no

  tasks:
  - name: Run system identification script
    command: /usr/bin/identify_system_specs
    register: system_info

  - name: Print system information
    debug: var=system_info.stdout_lines
```

In this playbook, we have defined a task that runs the C++ program on all the hosts defined in the inventory file. The register parameter is used to capture the output of the C++ program. We have defined another task to print the captured output.

We can run this playbook using the ansible-playbook command as follows:

```
$ ansible-playbook system_identification.yml -i inventory.ini
```

This will run the system identification script on all the hosts defined in the inventory.ini file and print the system information on the console.

Automating system identification using C++ and Ansible has several benefits. First, it reduces the manual effort required to identify the system specifications. Second, it ensures consistency in the system identification process across multiple devices. Third, it allows us to easily scale the system identification process as the network grows.

To summarize, automating system identification using a combination of C++ and Ansible is an important aspect of configuration management in networking. It allows us to efficiently and accurately identify the system specifications of multiple devices and ensures consistency in the process.

Automate System Patches and Updates

Automating system patches and updates is an important aspect of configuration management, as it helps to keep the system secure and up-to-date with the latest security patches and software updates. In this section, we will discuss how to automate system patches and updates using C++ and Ansible.

Install Ansible

The first step in automating system patches and updates is to install Ansible. Ansible is an open-source automation tool that can be used to manage and automate IT infrastructure. To install Ansible on a Linux system, follow these steps:

Open a terminal window on the Linux system.

Run the following command to install the EPEL repository:

```
sudo yum install epel-release
```

Run the following command to install Ansible:

```
sudo yum install ansible
```

Create Ansible Playbook

Once Ansible is installed, the next step is to create an Ansible playbook. An Ansible playbook is a script that defines a set of tasks to be performed on one or more systems. In this case, we will create a playbook that updates the system packages.

Open a text editor and create a new file named "update.yml".

Add the following code to the "update.yml" file:

```
---
- hosts: all
  become: yes
  tasks:
    - name: Update packages
```

```
yum:
  name: '*'
  state: latest
```

Save the file.

This Ansible playbook will update all the packages on the system to the latest version.

Execute Ansible Playbook

Once the Ansible playbook has been created, it can be executed to update the system packages.

Open a terminal window on the Linux system.

Navigate to the directory where the "update.yml" file is located.

Run the following command to execute the Ansible playbook:

```
ansible-playbook update.yml
```

This will execute the "update.yml" playbook and update all the packages on the system.

Automate Playbook with C++

To automate the process of running the Ansible playbook, we can use C++ to write a script that will execute the playbook on a scheduled basis.

Open a text editor and create a new file named "update.cpp".

Add the following code to the "update.cpp" file:

```
#include <stdlib.h>
int main() {
  system("ansible-playbook update.yml");
  return 0;
}
```

Save the file.

This C++ script will execute the "ansible-playbook update.yml" command, which will update all the packages on the system.

Schedule C++ Script

Once the C++ script has been created, it can be scheduled to run on a regular basis using the system's built-in scheduling tools, such as cron.

Open a terminal window on the Linux system.

Run the following command to open the crontab editor:

```
crontab -e
```

Add the following line to the crontab file to schedule the C++ script to run every week:

```
0 0 * * 0 /path/to/update.cpp
```

This will run the "update.cpp" script every Sunday at midnight.

Save the crontab file and exit the editor.

Now the system will automatically update all the packages every week, without any manual intervention.

In summary, automating system patches and updates is an important aspect of configuration management, and can be easily accomplished using C++ and Ansible. By creating an Ansible playbook and automating it with C++, we can ensure that our systems are always up-to-date.

Identify Unstable/Non-Compliant Configurations

To identify unstable and non-compliant configurations, you can use a combination of C++ and existing tools like Ansible or Puppet. Following is a practical demonstration of how to do this:

Define Configuration Baseline

First, you need to define a configuration baseline that represents the ideal state of your network environment. This baseline should include settings for all devices, services, and applications that are necessary for your network to function properly.

Use Ansible or Puppet to Collect Configuration Data

Next, you can use Ansible or Puppet to collect configuration data from all of the devices in your network environment. This can be done by writing a playbook or manifest that specifies the information you want to collect. For example, you might want to collect data on the settings for a particular application or service, or you might want to collect data on the configuration settings for a particular device.

Parse Collected Data with C++

Once you have collected the configuration data, you can parse it with C++ to identify any configurations that are unstable or non-compliant with your baseline. You can use C++ to compare the collected configuration data against your baseline and flag any configurations that do not match. For example, you might use C++ to check that all of your devices are running the correct version of the operating system, or that all of your applications are configured with the correct settings.

Generate Report

Once you have identified any unstable or non-compliant configurations, you can generate a report using C++. This report should include details on the configurations that are non-compliant, as well as recommendations for how to remediate these configurations. For example, you might recommend that a particular device be upgraded to the latest version of the operating system, or that a particular application be configured with a different set of settings.

Remediate Non-Compliant Configurations

Finally, you can use Ansible or Puppet to remediate any non-compliant configurations that you have identified. You can do this by writing a playbook or manifest that specifies the changes that need to be made to each device or application. For example, you might write a playbook that upgrades the operating system on a particular device or a manifest that configures a particular application with the correct settings.

In summary, by combining C++ with tools like Ansible or Puppet, you can automate the identification of unstable and non-compliant configurations in your network environment. This allows you to quickly identify any configurations that are causing problems or are not meeting your security requirements, and remediate these configurations automatically.

Sample Program

To identify unstable and non-compliant configurations, we can use C++ scripts to gather information about the network devices and configurations, and then use that information to compare against a standard baseline. The script can then identify any configurations that deviate from the baseline, and flag them as non-compliant or unstable.

Given below is a sample code that can be used to identify non-compliant configurations:

```
#include <iostream>
#include <string>
#include <vector>
#include <fstream>

using namespace std;

vector<string> getConfigurations(string deviceIP){
   vector<string> configurations;
   //connect to device and get configurations
   return configurations;
}

bool isNonCompliant(vector<string> configurations, string baselineConfig){
   bool isNonCompliant = false;
   //compare configurations against baseline
   //if configurations differ from baseline, set isNonCompliant to true
   return isNonCompliant;
}

int main(){
```

```
    string baselineConfig = "baseline_config.txt";
    vector<string> deviceIPs = {"192.168.1.1", "192.168.1.2", "192.168.1.3"};

    ofstream outfile;
    outfile.open("non_compliant_devices.txt");

    for(auto deviceIP : deviceIPs){
        vector<string> configurations = getConfigurations(deviceIP);
        if(isNonCompliant(configurations, baselineConfig)){
            outfile << deviceIP << endl;
        }
    }

    outfile.close();

    return 0;
}
```

In this code, we first define a function getConfigurations that connects to a device with a given IP address and retrieves its configurations. We then define a function isNonCompliant that compares the configurations against a baseline configuration file and returns true if they differ.

In the main function, we define the baseline configuration file and a list of device IP addresses. We then loop through each device, retrieve its configurations, and check if they are non-compliant. If a device is non-compliant, we write its IP address to a file called non_compliant_devices.txt.

This is just one example of how C++ can be used to identify non-compliant configurations. The specific implementation will depend on the network environment and the types of configurations that need to be checked.

Summary

In this chapter, we discussed various aspects of configuration management using Ansible and C++ automation. We first explained the importance of configuration management and the benefits of automating it using C++.

We then discussed server provisioning, which involves setting up and configuring new servers for use. We demonstrated how to automate this process using C++ tools, including code snippets for performing tasks such as installing packages, setting up user accounts, and configuring network interfaces. We also discussed the use of Ansible for server provisioning and demonstrated how to use Ansible playbooks to automate the process.

Next, we discussed automating system settings, which involves setting up and configuring various system-level settings. We demonstrated how to do this using C++ code snippets, including examples of modifying system settings such as the system hostname and timezone.

We then discussed modifying base configurations and demonstrated how to do this using C++ and optionally using Ansible. We explained that base configurations are a set of configurations that are common across multiple systems and demonstrated how to modify them using C++ code snippets and Ansible playbooks.

Next, we discussed automating system identification and demonstrated how to do this using a combination of C++ and Ansible. We explained that system identification involves identifying various attributes of a system, such as its hostname, IP address, and MAC address.

We then discussed automating system patches and updates, which involves keeping the system up to date with the latest patches and updates. We demonstrated how to do this using C++ code snippets, including examples of using the apt package manager to install updates.

Finally, we discussed identifying unstable and non-compliant configurations and demonstrated how to do this using C++ code snippets. We explained that this involves scanning the system for various security vulnerabilities and non-compliant configurations.

Overall, this chapter provided a comprehensive overview of configuration management using Ansible and C++ automation, covering a wide range of topics including server provisioning, system settings, base configurations, system identification, patches and updates, and identifying unstable configurations. We also provided practical demonstrations and code snippets to help readers understand how to perform these tasks in practice.

Chapter 6: Working with Docker and Containers

Exploring Docker and Containers

Overview

Docker is a popular tool for containerization and virtualization that has revolutionized the way applications are deployed and managed. It enables developers to package their applications and dependencies into a single, lightweight container that can be deployed on any platform without requiring any additional configuration.

A container is a lightweight, standalone, and executable package of software that contains everything needed to run an application, including the application code, libraries, and system tools. It provides a consistent environment for running an application regardless of the underlying system, making it ideal for building, testing, and deploying applications in a wide variety of environments.

Role of C++ in Containerization

C++ plays an important role in Docker and containerization as it is used for networking and communication between containers and the host system. C++ provides a fast and efficient way of handling network traffic and can be used to develop high-performance networking applications.

Containers are designed to be lightweight and portable, and as such, they typically have minimal networking components. This is where C++ comes in, as it provides the necessary networking components that enable containers to communicate with each other and the host system.

C++ provides a rich set of libraries and tools that can be used for networking, including Boost.Asio, ZeroMQ, and RESTbed. These libraries provide an easy-to-use interface for developing high-performance networking applications, allowing developers to focus on building their applications without having to worry about the low-level networking details.

C++ also provides support for containerization and virtualization through tools such as Docker and Kubernetes. These tools enable developers to create, deploy, and manage containerized applications in a highly scalable and efficient manner. They provide a consistent environment for running applications across multiple platforms, making it easier to develop and deploy applications across different environments.

Benefits of C++ For Docker and Containers

Using C++ for networking in Docker and containers has many benefits, including:

High performance: C++ provides a fast and efficient way of handling network traffic, enabling applications to perform at peak levels.

Scalability: C++ networking libraries and tools are highly scalable, allowing developers to build applications that can handle large volumes of traffic and scale up or down as needed.

Portability: C++ networking components can be easily ported to different platforms and architectures, making it easier to develop and deploy applications across different environments.

Flexibility: C++ provides a wide range of networking libraries and tools that can be used for different purposes, making it easy to tailor applications to specific requirements.

To summarize, C++ plays a critical role in Docker and containerization by providing the necessary networking components that enable containers to communicate with each other and the host system. Its high performance, scalability, portability, and flexibility make it an ideal choice for developing high-performance networking applications for containerized environments.

Types of Docker Networks

Docker is a popular platform for building, shipping, and running containerized applications. One of the key features of Docker is its networking capabilities, which enable containers to communicate with each other and with the outside world. In this context, a Docker network is a virtual network that connects a set of containers and provides them with an isolated environment for communication. In this section, we will describe Docker networks and their different types.

Docker provides four types of networks: bridge, host, overlay, and macvlan. Each of these networks has its own characteristics and use cases.

Bridge Network

The bridge network is the default network type in Docker. It allows containers to communicate with each other and with the outside world using the Docker daemon as a gateway. When a container is created, it is assigned an IP address on the bridge network, and can communicate with other containers on the same network by using this IP address. This network type is suitable for most applications, as it provides a good balance between isolation and connectivity.

Host Network

In the host network type, the containers are directly connected to the host network interface, and they share the same network stack as the host. This means that containers on the host network can communicate with the host and with other devices on the same network as the host. The host network type provides the best performance and lowest latency, but it does not provide any isolation between containers.

Overlay Network

The overlay network type is used for connecting multiple Docker hosts together, allowing containers on different hosts to communicate with each other as if they were on the same network. This network type is useful for distributed applications that are running on multiple hosts, and it provides a high degree of isolation and security between the containers.

Macvlan Network

The macvlan network type allows containers to be directly connected to a physical network interface on the host, and each container is assigned a unique MAC address. This network type is useful for applications that require direct access to the network, such as network monitoring or packet capture tools. It provides the highest degree of isolation and security between containers, but it requires more configuration and management than the other network types.

In summary, Docker provides four types of networks: bridge, host, overlay, and macvlan. Each network type has its own characteristics and use cases, and the choice of network type depends on the requirements of the application.

Install and Configure Docker

Following are the steps to install Docker and configure it for C++:

Install Docker

First, you need to install Docker on your system. You can download the installation package from the official Docker website. Follow the instructions provided for your operating system to install Docker.

Test Docker Installation

After the installation is complete, verify that Docker is installed correctly by running the following command in the terminal:

```
docker version
```

This command will display the version information for both the Docker client and server.

Configure Docker for C++

To configure Docker for C++, you need to create a Dockerfile. A Dockerfile is a text file that contains all the instructions to build a Docker image. The Docker image is a lightweight, standalone, executable package that includes everything needed to run an application, including the application code, runtime, system tools, libraries, and settings.

Given below is an example Dockerfile that configures Docker for C++:

```
# Use an official C++ runtime as a parent image
FROM gcc:latest

# Set the working directory to /app
WORKDIR /app

# Copy the current directory contents into the container at /app
COPY . /app

# Compile the source code
RUN g++ -o app main.cpp

# Set the command to run the executable
CMD ["./app"]
```

This Dockerfile creates a Docker image that uses the latest version of the GCC compiler as the base image, sets the working directory to /app, copies the source code to the container, compiles the code using g++, and sets the command to run the executable.

To build the Docker image, navigate to the directory where the Dockerfile is saved and run the following command:

```
docker build -t myapp .
```

This command will build the Docker image and tag it with the name "myapp".

Once the image is built, you can run the container using the following command:

```
docker run myapp
```

This command will start the container and execute the application.

Test Docker Container

To test the Docker container, you can create a simple C++ program that prints "Hello, world!" to the console. Save the following code to a file named "main.cpp":

```
#include <iostream>

int main() {
   std::cout << "Hello, world!" << std::endl;
   return 0;
}
```

Then, copy this file to the directory where you created the Dockerfile.

After running the "docker build" and "docker run" commands as described above, you should see "Hello, world!" printed to the console. This indicates that the Docker container has been successfully configured for C++ and the application is running correctly.

In summary, to install and configure Docker for C++, you need to first install Docker on your system, create a Dockerfile that contains the necessary configuration settings, build the Docker image, and then run the container to execute the application. By following these steps, you can easily set up a Docker environment for your C++ applications and enjoy the benefits of containerization, such as portability, scalability, and isolation.

Build Docker Images

Docker images are the building blocks of containers in Docker. They contain all the necessary components of a containerized application, including the code, runtime, system tools, libraries, and settings. Docker images are created using a Dockerfile, which is a text file that contains instructions for building the image.

To build a Docker image for a C++ application, we need to follow these steps:

Create Dockerfile

We first need to create a Dockerfile that contains the instructions for building the Docker image. The Dockerfile should be located in the root directory of the C++ application. Given below is an example Dockerfile for a C++ application:

```
FROM ubuntu:latest

RUN apt-get update && \
    apt-get install -y g++ && \
    apt-get clean

COPY . /app

WORKDIR /app

RUN g++ -o app main.cpp

CMD ["./app"]
```

This Dockerfile starts with the latest Ubuntu image, installs the g++ compiler, copies the C++ application code to the /app directory, compiles the code using g++, and sets the command to run the compiled application.

Build Docker Image

Once we have created the Dockerfile, we can build the Docker image using the docker build command. We need to run this command in the same directory as the Dockerfile.

```
docker build -t my-cpp-app .
```

This command builds the Docker image using the Dockerfile in the current directory and tags it with the name "my-cpp-app".

Run Docker Container

Once we have built the Docker image, we can run the Docker container using the docker run command.

```
docker run my-cpp-app
```

This command runs the Docker container using the "my-cpp-app" image that we built earlier.

Note: Before running the Docker container, make sure that you have installed Docker on your system and that it is running properly.

In summary, to build a Docker image for a C++ application, we need to create a Dockerfile with the necessary instructions, build the image using the docker build command, and run the container using the docker run command.

Run Containers

Running containers in Docker means starting an instance of a Docker image as a container on a Docker host. When a container is started, it runs in its own isolated environment with its own file system, networking, and resources, and can be easily stopped, started, or destroyed.

Following is a practical demonstration of running a container using Docker:

First, we need to pull a Docker image from a registry. For this demonstration, we'll use the official nginx image. Open a terminal and run the following command:

```
docker pull nginx
```

This command will download the latest nginx image from the Docker Hub registry.

Once the image is downloaded, we can run it as a container using the following command:

```
docker run -d -p 80:80 nginx
```

This command will start a container in detached mode (-d) with port mapping (-p) from the container's port 80 to the host's port 80. We're also specifying the nginx image to run.

To check if the container is running, we can run the following command:

```
docker ps
```

This command will list all running containers. You should see the nginx container listed along with its container ID, image name, and other details.

Now that the container is running, we can access it by opening a web browser and navigating to http://localhost. You should see the default nginx page displayed.

To stop the container, we can use the following command:

```
docker stop <container-id>
```

Replace <container-id> with the ID of the nginx container listed in the docker ps command.

To remove the container, use the following command:

```
docker rm <container-id>
```

Replace <container-id> with the ID of the nginx container listed in the docker ps -a command.

The -a option lists all containers, including stopped ones.

By following these steps, we can easily run Docker containers and test our applications in isolated environments.

Automate Running Containers

Automating the running of containers involves creating scripts that can be executed to start and stop containers automatically. This can be achieved using various tools and scripting languages, including C++.

To automate the running of containers with C++, you can use the Docker SDK for C++. The Docker SDK for C++ is a library that provides a C++ interface for interacting with the Docker Engine API.

Following are the steps to automate the running of containers using C++:

Install Docker SDK for C++

You can install the Docker SDK for C++ by downloading the source code from the official GitHub repository and building it on your system.

Include Docker SDK in C++ Project

Once you have installed the Docker SDK for C++, you need to include the appropriate header files and link the library to your C++ project.

Write C++ Code to Start and Stop Containers

You can use the Docker SDK for C++ to write C++ code that starts and stops containers. Given below is a sample code snippet that starts a container using the Docker SDK for C++:

```
#include <iostream>
#include <chrono>
#include <thread>
#include <docker.hpp>

int main()
{
    docker::Docker docker;

    // Create a container configuration
    docker::ContainerConfig config;
    config.Image = "nginx";
    config.Name = "my-nginx-container";
```

```
    config.PortBindings["80/tcp"].push_back({"0.0.0.0", 8080});

    // Create the container
    docker::Container container = docker.createContainer(config);

    // Start the container
    container.start();

    // Wait for the container to start up
    std::cout << "Waiting for container to start up...\n";
    std::this_thread::sleep_for(std::chrono::seconds(5));

    // Stop the container
    container.stop();

    return 0;
}
```

This code snippet creates a Docker container based on the Nginx image, binds port 80 to port 8080 on the host, starts the container, waits for it to start up, and then stops the container.

Build and Run C++ Project

Once you have written the C++ code to start and stop containers, you need to build the C++ project and run the executable to start and stop containers automatically.

Hence, automating the running of containers with C++ involves using the Docker SDK for C++ to write C++ code that starts and stops containers, and then building and running the C++ project to start and stop containers automatically.

Manage Container Networks

Managing container networks is an important aspect of container orchestration as it allows containers to communicate with each other and with other networks. Docker provides several options for managing container networks.

Default Network

By default, Docker creates a bridge network for containers to connect to. This network allows containers to communicate with each other and with the host system. To create a new container on this network, simply specify the --network flag when running the container.

Custom Network

Docker also allows the creation of custom networks, which can be used to isolate containers from each other and from the host system. Custom networks can be created using the docker network create command.

For example, to create a custom network named my_network, run the following command:

```
$ docker network create my_network
```

Once the network is created, containers can be attached to it using the --network flag when running the container.

External Network

Docker also provides the option to connect containers to external networks, such as a physical network interface or a virtual private network (VPN). To connect a container to an external network, create the network using the appropriate tool and then attach the container to the network using the --network flag.

For example, to connect a container to an external network named my_external_network, run the following command:

```
$ docker run --network=my_external_network my_image
```

Overlay Network

Docker also supports overlay networks, which can be used to connect containers across multiple hosts. Overlay networks can be created using Docker swarm mode.

To create an overlay network named my_overlay_network, run the following command:

```
$ docker network create --driver=overlay my_overlay_network
```

Once the network is created, containers can be attached to it using the --network flag when running the container.

Docker Network Commands

To manage container networks, Docker provides several commands, including:

- docker network ls: Lists all available networks.
- docker network create: Creates a new network.
- docker network connect: Connects a container to a network.
- docker network disconnect: Disconnects a container from a network.
- docker network inspect: Displays detailed information about a network.
- docker network rm: Removes a network.

How to Use Docker Commands

To practically manage container networks in Docker, follow these steps:

List available networks

Use the docker network ls command to list all available networks.

```
$ docker network ls
```

Create a new network

Use the docker network create command to create a new network.

```
$ docker network create my_network
```

Attach a container to a network

Use the --network flag when running a container to attach it to a network.

```
$ docker run --network=my_network my_image
```

Disconnect a container from a network

Use the docker network disconnect command to disconnect a container from a network.

```
$ docker network disconnect my_network my_container
```

Display detailed information about a network
Use the docker network inspect command to display detailed information about a network.

```
$ docker network inspect my_network
```

Remove a network
Use the docker network rm command to remove a network.

```
$ docker network rm my_network
```

By managing container networks in Docker, containers can communicate with each other and with external networks, which is essential for building complex applications using containers.

Summary

In this chapter, we discussed Docker and its role in modern software development. We started by discussing the concept of containers, which are lightweight, portable, and self-contained environments that can run applications and services. Containers have become increasingly popular because they allow developers to package their applications along with all of their dependencies and configurations, which makes it easier to deploy and manage them across different environments.

Next, we discussed Docker networks, which are virtual networks that allow containers to communicate with each other and with the outside world. There are several types of Docker networks, including bridge networks, overlay networks, and macvlan networks. We discussed each type in detail and provided examples of when to use them.

We then moved on to the practical aspects of using Docker. We discussed the steps to install Docker on a Linux system, including how to configure it for C++ development. We then discussed Docker images, which are the building blocks of containers. We provided a step-by-step demonstration of how to build a Docker image for a C++ application.
After that, we discussed how to run containers using Docker. We provided a demonstration of how to run a container from a Docker image and how to access it from the host system.

We then discussed automation in Docker, which involves using tools like Docker Compose and Kubernetes to manage containers and orchestrate them across different environments. We provided a brief overview of these tools and their capabilities.

Finally, we discussed the importance of managing Docker networks and how to do so using the Docker CLI. We demonstrated how to create, inspect, and delete Docker networks.

In summary, this chapter covered the basics of Docker and containers, including installation and configuration, building Docker images, running containers, and managing container networks. We also touched on automation and orchestration, which are important considerations for managing large-scale container deployments. With the help of these practical demonstrations, readers should have a good understanding of how to use Docker and containers in their C++ development workflow.

CHAPTER 7: CONTAINER ORCHESTRATION AND WORKLOAD AUTOMATION

Understanding Container Scheduling

Container scheduling is a method of managing the deployment and scaling of containers across a cluster of nodes or servers. Container orchestration tools, such as Kubernetes or Docker Swarm, provide a means of automating the deployment and management of containerized applications across multiple hosts or machines.

In a containerized environment, applications are packaged and run within containers, which are portable and can be easily moved between different environments. Container orchestration tools provide a way to manage these containers and ensure that they are running efficiently and effectively.

Container scheduling involves several key components, including resource allocation, load balancing, and scaling. Resource allocation ensures that containers are running on the appropriate nodes and that they have the necessary resources to operate efficiently. Load balancing ensures that network traffic is distributed evenly across the available nodes, reducing the likelihood of overloading any one node. Scaling ensures that additional containers can be deployed or removed as needed, depending on changes in demand or other factors.

Network automation can provide several benefits to container orchestration, including:

Automated configuration: By automating network configuration, it becomes easier to deploy and manage containers across multiple hosts or machines. Network automation tools can ensure that network settings are configured consistently and accurately across all nodes in the cluster.

Dynamic scaling: Network automation can be used to automatically adjust network configurations as containers are added or removed from the cluster. This ensures that the network is always optimized for the current load and that resources are used efficiently.

Self-healing: Network automation can be used to automatically detect and correct network failures, reducing downtime and ensuring that the cluster remains operational.

Enhanced security: Network automation can be used to automatically configure security settings and apply security policies across the entire cluster. This ensures that the network is secure and that containers are protected from external threats.

In summary, container scheduling is a critical component of container orchestration, and network automation can provide several benefits to the process. By automating network configuration, scaling, and security, container orchestration becomes more efficient, reliable, and secure.

What is Service Discovery?

Service discovery is the process by which a system or a software component can automatically find and locate other services or resources that it needs to function. In a distributed computing environment, where services can be deployed across different nodes or machines, service discovery helps to simplify the process of finding and communicating with these services.

In a service-oriented architecture (SOA) or microservices architecture, services are typically deployed in containers or virtual machines. Service discovery helps to manage these services by providing a way for containers or VMs to find and connect with each other. It allows services to be added or removed dynamically without manual intervention, and enables load balancing and failover mechanisms to be implemented.

There are several approaches to implementing service discovery, including:

DNS-Based Service Discovery

In this approach, each service is assigned a domain name, and a DNS server is used to map the domain name to the IP address of the container or virtual machine where the service is running. When a client needs to connect to a service, it queries the DNS server for the IP address of the service.

Client-Side Service Discovery

In this approach, each client has a local registry of available services, and is responsible for querying the registry to find the IP address of the service it needs to connect to. The registry is typically populated by a service registry or discovery service, which keeps track of the available services.

Server-Side Service Discovery

In this approach, a central service registry or discovery service maintains a list of available services and their locations, and clients query the registry to find the IP address of the service they need to connect to.

Service discovery plays an important role in container orchestration platforms like Kubernetes, which is designed to manage containerized applications and services at scale. Kubernetes uses a combination of DNS-based and client-side service discovery to manage service discovery and load balancing for containers. Network automation can help to streamline the process of configuring and managing Kubernetes clusters, ensuring that containers can be easily discovered and connected to each other.

Process of Service Discovery Automation

Automating service discovery refers to the process of automatically discovering and registering services within a network environment. This is typically done by using a service registry or discovery tool, which allows services to register themselves and provides a mechanism for other services to discover and communicate with them.

In order to automate service discovery with C++, there are a number of tools and libraries that can be used, such as Consul, etcd, and Zookeeper. These tools provide a centralized mechanism for discovering and managing services within a network environment, and can be integrated with C++ code using APIs and libraries provided by the respective tools.

Following is the ultimate practical demonstration of how to automate service discovery with C++ using Consul as an example:

Install and Configure Consul

The first step is to install and configure Consul on your network environment. This involves setting up a Consul server and configuring it to work with your network infrastructure.

Create Service

Next, you will need to create a service that can be discovered and registered by Consul. This can be done using C++ code that defines the service, including its name, IP address, and any other relevant metadata.

Register Service

Once the service is defined, it can be registered with Consul using the Consul API. This involves sending a registration request to the Consul server, which will then add the service to its registry.

Discover Service

Once the service is registered, it can be discovered by other services within the network using the Consul API. This involves sending a discovery request to the Consul server, which will return information about the available services that match the specified criteria.

Communicate With Service

Once the service has been discovered, other services can communicate with it using the IP address and port number provided by Consul. This can be done using C++ code that sends and receives messages to and from the service.

Overall, automating service discovery with C++ and tools like Consul can help to simplify the management and communication of services within a network environment. By providing a centralized mechanism for registering and discovering services, these tools can make it easier to build and maintain complex distributed systems.

Using C++ to Automate Service Discovery

Suppose we have a microservices-based application that consists of multiple services, and we want to automate the service discovery process. We can use C++ and its networking libraries, along with a service discovery tool such as Consul, to achieve this.

Following are the steps to demonstrate how to automate service discovery with C++ and Consul:

Install Consul

First, we need to install Consul on our system or server. Consul is a tool that provides service discovery, health checking, and key-value storage functionalities. It can be easily installed on Linux, macOS, and Windows systems.

Register Services

Next, we need to register our services with Consul. We can use the Consul API or command-line interface (CLI) to register services. For example, we can use the following command to register a service named "user-service" with Consul:

```
$ consul services register -name=user-service -address=127.0.0.1 -port=8000
```

This command registers the "user-service" with the IP address of 127.0.0.1 and port number of 8000.

Query Services

After registering the services, we can query the services using the Consul API or CLI. For example, we can use the following command to list all the services registered with Consul:

```
$ consul catalog services
```

This command lists all the services registered with Consul along with their names and tags.

Integrate with C++ code

Finally, we can integrate the service discovery functionality with our C++ code. We can use C++ networking libraries such as Boost.Asio or C++ REST SDK to communicate with the Consul API and query the registered services.

Sample Program to Query Registered Services using Boost.Asio

```
#include <iostream>
#include <boost/asio.hpp>

using namespace std;
using boost::asio::ip::tcp;

int main()
{
   try {
      boost::asio::io_context io_context;

      // Connect to Consul HTTP API
      tcp::resolver resolver(io_context);
      tcp::socket socket(io_context);
      tcp::resolver::results_type    endpoints    =    resolver.resolve("localhost",
```

```
"8500");
    boost::asio::connect(socket, endpoints);

    // Send query request to Consul
    boost::asio::streambuf request;
    ostream request_stream(&request);
    request_stream << "GET /v1/catalog/services HTTP/1.1\r\n";
    request_stream << "Host: localhost\r\n";
    request_stream << "Accept: */*\r\n";
    request_stream << "Connection: close\r\n\r\n";
    boost::asio::write(socket, request);

    // Read response from Consul
    boost::asio::streambuf response;
    boost::asio::read_until(socket, response, "\r\n\r\n");
    istream response_stream(&response);
    string http_version;
    response_stream >> http_version;
    unsigned int status_code;
    response_stream >> status_code;

    // Parse and print service names
    string line;
    while (getline(response_stream, line)) {
        if (line.size() > 0) {
            size_t pos = line.find(":");
            if (pos != string::npos) {
                string key = line.substr(0, pos);
                string value = line.substr(pos+1);
                if (key == "ServiceName") {
                    cout << "Service: " << value << endl;
                }
```

```
        }
    }
}

// Close connection
boost::system::
```

Define Environment Variables

In this step, we will define the environment variables that will be used by the service discovery script. We will create a .env file in the root directory of the project and define the following environment variables:

```
REDIS_HOST=redis
REDIS_PORT=6379
```

Write Service Discovery Script

Now, we will write the C++ script that will perform the service discovery task. We will create a service_discovery.cpp file in the src directory of the project and write the following code:

```
#include <iostream>
#include <hiredis/hiredis.h>
#include <cstdlib>

int main() {
    const char *redis_host = std::getenv("REDIS_HOST");
    const char *redis_port = std::getenv("REDIS_PORT");

    redisContext *c;
    redisReply *reply;

    c = redisConnect(redis_host, std::atoi(redis_port));
```

```
    if (c == NULL || c->err) {
        std::cerr << "Error connecting to Redis: " << c->errstr << std::endl;
        exit(1);
    }

    reply = (redisReply*) redisCommand(c, "KEYS *");
    if (reply == NULL || reply->type != REDIS_REPLY_ARRAY) {
        std::cerr << "Error executing command: " << c->errstr << std::endl;
        exit(1);
    }

    for (int i = 0; i < reply->elements; i++) {
        std::cout << reply->element[i]->str << std::endl;
    }

    freeReplyObject(reply);
    redisFree(c);

    return 0;
}
```

This script will connect to the Redis server using the environment variables defined in the .env file, execute the KEYS * command to retrieve all the keys in the Redis database, and print them to the console.

Build Project

Now, we will build the project by running the following command in the root directory of the project:

```
docker-compose build
```

This command will build the Docker image for the C++ application using the Dockerfile defined earlier.

Start Containers

Finally, we will start the containers by running the following command:

```
docker-compose up
```

This command will start the Redis container and the C++ application container. The C++ application container will connect to the Redis container and retrieve the keys from the database using the service_discovery.cpp script.

Test Service Discovery

To test the service discovery, we can run the following command:

```
docker exec -it service-discovery /bin/bash
```

This command will open a Bash shell in the C++ application container. We can then run the ./service_discovery command to retrieve the keys from the Redis database.

If everything is working correctly, we should see the keys printed to the console.

Clean Up

To clean up the containers and the Docker network, we can run the following command in the root directory of the project:

```
docker-compose down
```

This command will stop and remove the containers and the Docker network.

In summary, automating service discovery with C++ can greatly simplify the process of discovering and connecting to services in a distributed system. By using a combination of C++ libraries and Docker containers, we can create a robust and scalable service discovery system that can easily be integrated into any application.

Necessity of Load Balancers

Load balancers are an essential component of modern computer networking infrastructure. A load balancer is a device or software that distributes incoming network traffic across multiple servers to ensure that no one server is overwhelmed with requests. Load balancing can be done on various levels, such as at the network layer, the transport layer, or the application layer.

Working Principles

The basic working principle of load balancers involves receiving requests from clients, analyzing these requests, and then routing them to the most appropriate server in the pool of available servers. This analysis may take into account factors such as server load, server proximity, or the nature of the request itself. The load balancer then forwards the request to the chosen server, which processes it and sends the response back to the client through the load balancer.

Load balancing can be implemented using various algorithms, such as round-robin, weighted round-robin, least connections, or IP hash. These algorithms determine how requests are distributed among the available servers, and they can be customized to suit specific network requirements.

Benefits of Load Balancing

Load balancers can provide several benefits to network infrastructure, including improved availability, scalability, and reliability. By distributing incoming traffic among multiple servers, load balancers can ensure that no one server becomes overloaded or fails, thus reducing the risk of downtime or service disruption. Additionally, load balancers can make it easier to scale out network infrastructure by adding more servers to the pool as needed, without affecting the overall performance or reliability of the system.

Overall, load balancers are an essential tool for managing network traffic and ensuring high levels of availability, scalability, and reliability in modern computer networking infrastructure.

Automatng Load Balancing Management

Network automation plays a crucial role in load balancing management. Load balancing is a critical task in a network environment where multiple servers or resources are available to serve requests. Load balancers distribute incoming network traffic across multiple servers to ensure optimal performance, high availability, and scalability.

Network automation can help manage and automate load balancers by providing a centralized way to configure and manage them. Automation scripts can be used to configure load balancers, set up rules for distributing traffic, monitor the health of the servers, and perform maintenance tasks.

For example, automation scripts can be used to automatically add or remove servers from a load balancer based on their availability or performance metrics. They can also be used to configure load balancing algorithms, set up SSL certificates, and configure health checks.

By automating load balancing management, network administrators can ensure that their network is always running at peak performance, reduce the risk of human error, and improve the efficiency of their network operations.

Add or Remove Servers from Load Balancer

To write an automation script to automatically add or remove servers from a load balancer based on their availability or performance metrics in C++, we can follow the following steps:

Install Necessary Libraries and Tools

We need to install the following libraries and tools:

- The Load Balancer API library
- The Server Management API library
- The Performance Metrics API library
- The C++ programming language
- A text editor or an integrated development environment (IDE) to write the code

Define Variables

We need to define the following variables:

- The load balancer ID
- The server IDs
- The performance metrics threshold

Connect to Load Balancer API

We need to connect to the Load Balancer API using the API key and secret.

Retrieve Server Information

We need to retrieve the information of all the servers in the load balancer.

Calculate Performance Metrics

We need to calculate the performance metrics for each server, such as the server response time or the server availability.

Check Performance Metrics

We need to check if the performance metrics of each server are below the threshold.

Add or Remove Servers from Load Balancer

Based on the performance metrics, we need to add or remove the servers from the load balancer.

Repeat Process

We need to repeat the process at a regular interval to ensure that the load balancer is always optimized.

Sample Program

Following is a sample code that implements the above steps:

```
#include <iostream>
#include <loadbalancerapi.h>
#include <servermanagementapi.h>
#include <performancemetricsapi.h>

using namespace std;

// Define the variables
const string LB_ID = "lb123";
const vector<string> SERVER_IDS = {"server1", "server2", "server3"};
const double PERFORMANCE_METRICS_THRESHOLD = 0.5;

int main() {
  // Connect to the Load Balancer API
  LoadBalancerAPI lbAPI("api_key", "api_secret");
```

```
    // Retrieve the server information
    vector<Server> servers = lbAPI.getServers(LB_ID);

    // Calculate the performance metrics
    PerformanceMetricsAPI pmAPI("api_key", "api_secret");
    for (Server server : servers) {
        double responseTime = pmAPI.getResponseTime(server.id);
        double availability = pmAPI.getAvailability(server.id);
        double performanceMetrics = (1 - responseTime) * availability;
        server.performanceMetrics = performanceMetrics;
    }

    // Add or remove servers from the load balancer
    ServerManagementAPI smAPI("api_key", "api_secret");
    for (Server server : servers) {
        if                          (server.performanceMetrics                          <
PERFORMANCE_METRICS_THRESHOLD) {
            smAPI.removeServer(LB_ID, server.id);
        } else {
            smAPI.addServer(LB_ID, server.id);
        }
    }

    return 0;
}
```

This program uses the Load Balancer API, the Server Management API, and the Performance Metrics API to retrieve the server information, calculate the performance metrics, and add or remove servers from the load balancer. The program defines the load balancer ID, the server IDs, and the performance metrics threshold as variables and uses them in the program. The program also connects to the APIs using the API key and secret.

Configure Load Balancing Algorithms

To configure load balancing algorithms using C++, we can use a library called the "Load Balance Manager" library. This library provides functions to set up different load balancing algorithms like round-robin, least-connections, IP hash, and others.

Following is a sample C++ code that demonstrates how to configure a load balancer with the round-robin algorithm:

```
#include <lbm.h> // Load Balance Manager library

int main()
{
  // create a new load balancer instance
  lbm_handle_t lbm;
  lbm_init(&lbm);

  // set the algorithm to round-robin
  lbm_set_algorithm(lbm, LBM_ALGO_ROUND_ROBIN);

  // add servers to the load balancer
  lbm_add_server(lbm, "10.0.0.1", 80);
  lbm_add_server(lbm, "10.0.0.2", 80);
  lbm_add_server(lbm, "10.0.0.3", 80);

  // configure the load balancer
  lbm_set_max_connections(lbm, 1000);
  lbm_set_timeout(lbm, 5);

  // start the load balancer
  lbm_start(lbm);

  // use the load balancer to send requests
  // ...
```

```
    // stop the load balancer
    lbm_stop(lbm);

    // clean up
    lbm_cleanup(lbm);

    return 0;
}
```

In the above sample program, we first create a new load balancer instance using the lbm_init() function. We then set the load balancing algorithm to round-robin using the lbm_set_algorithm() function. Next, we add three servers to the load balancer using the lbm_add_server() function.

We then configure the load balancer with a maximum number of connections and a timeout using the lbm_set_max_connections() and lbm_set_timeout() functions, respectively. After configuring the load balancer, we start it using the lbm_start() function.

We can then use the load balancer to send requests to the servers. Finally, we stop the load balancer using the lbm_stop() function and clean up the load balancer instance using the lbm_cleanup() function.

Automate Setting Up SSL Certificates

Following is a practical example of automating the process of setting up SSL certificates using C++:

Include The Necessary Headers

```
#include <iostream>
#include <string>
#include <openssl/ssl.h>
#include <openssl/err.h>
```

Initialize Ssl Library

Next, we need to define a function to initialize the SSL library and load the SSL certificates:

```
int init_ssl()
{
  SSL_library_init();
  SSL_load_error_strings();
  ERR_load_BIO_strings();
  OpenSSL_add_all_algorithms();

  SSL_CTX *ctx = SSL_CTX_new(SSLv23_server_method());

  if (!ctx)
  {
    std::cerr << "Error initializing SSL context" << std::endl;
    return -1;
  }

  if          (SSL_CTX_use_certificate_file(ctx,          "/path/to/certificate.crt",
SSL_FILETYPE_PEM) <= 0)
  {
    std::cerr << "Error loading certificate file" << std::endl;
    return -1;
  }

  if          (SSL_CTX_use_PrivateKey_file(ctx,          "/path/to/private.key",
SSL_FILETYPE_PEM) <= 0)
  {
    std::cerr << "Error loading private key file" << std::endl;
    return -1;
  }
```

```
    if (!SSL_CTX_check_private_key(ctx))
    {
        std::cerr << "Error checking private key" << std::endl;
        return -1;
    }

    return 0;
}
```

This function initializes the SSL library, creates a new SSL context, and loads the SSL certificate and private key files.

Putting Function into Action

We can then use this function in our main program:

```
int main()
{
    if (init_ssl() != 0)
    {
        std::cerr << "Error initializing SSL" << std::endl;
        return -1;
    }

    // Other code here

    return 0;
}
```

By calling the init_ssl() function at the beginning of our program, we ensure that the SSL library is properly initialized and the SSL certificates are loaded.

Purpose of Container Storage

Container storage is a concept that refers to the storage of data within a container environment. When a container is created, it includes all of the necessary libraries, binaries, and configuration files needed to run the application or service it contains. These containers can be ephemeral, meaning that they can be created and destroyed as needed, or they can be long-lived.

In the context of container storage, there are two main types of storage: ephemeral and persistent. Ephemeral storage is storage that is created when a container is created and destroyed when the container is destroyed. This type of storage is typically used for temporary files, caches, or other types of data that do not need to be persisted beyond the lifecycle of the container.

Persistent storage, on the other hand, is storage that is not tied to the lifecycle of a container. It can be used to store data that needs to persist beyond the lifecycle of a container, such as application data, databases, and other important files.

In order to manage container storage effectively, it is important to have a strategy in place for managing both ephemeral and persistent storage. This can include using volume mounts to mount host directories or network file systems to containers, using storage plugins to manage storage on external storage systems, or using storage orchestration tools to manage storage at scale.

Overall, container storage plays a critical role in container-based environments, as it allows containers to store and access data in a way that is efficient, scalable, and flexible. By using a combination of tools, technologies, and best practices, organizations can effectively manage container storage and ensure that their applications and services have access to the data they need to operate effectively.

Manage Container Storage

Managing container storage is a critical aspect of containerization. Containers need storage to function, and they generate data that needs to be stored persistently. Container storage can be managed in several ways, including using container storage drivers, using external storage providers, or using container data volumes. In this demonstration, we will focus on using container data volumes to manage container storage.

To manage container storage using container data volumes in C++, we will use the Docker C++ SDK library. The Docker C++ SDK is a C++ library that provides a convenient and easy-to-use interface for working with the Docker API.

Create Container with Data Volume

The following is a sample C++ program that demonstrates how to create a container with a data volume, mount the data volume to a directory in the container, and write data to the data volume:

```
#include <iostream>
#include <docker/client.hpp>
#include <docker/types.hpp>

int main() {
    docker::client cli{ "unix:///var/run/docker.sock" };

    // create the data volume
    docker::types::volume_create_opts opts;
    opts.set_name("my-data-volume");
    docker::types::volume vol = cli.volumes().create(opts);

    // create the container
    docker::types::container_create_opts container_opts;
    container_opts.set_image("my-image");
    container_opts.set_name("my-container");
    container_opts.add_mount(docker::types::mount{
        .type = docker::types::mount_type::VOLUME,
        .source = vol.name(),
        .target = "/data"
    });
    docker::types::container container = cli.containers().create(container_opts);

    // start the container
    docker::types::container_start_opts start_opts;
    cli.containers().start(container.id(), start_opts);
```

```
    // write data to the data volume
    docker::types::container_exec_create_opts exec_opts;
    exec_opts.set_cmd({ "sh", "-c", "echo 'Hello, world!' > /data/hello.txt" });
    docker::types::container_exec exec =
cli.containers().exec_create(container.id(), exec_opts);
    docker::types::container_exec_start_opts exec_start_opts;
    std::string output = cli.containers().exec_start(exec.id(), exec_start_opts);

    std::cout << "Output: " << output << std::endl;

    return 0;
}
```

In this program, we first create a data volume named "my-data-volume" using the docker::types::volume_create_opts class. We then create a container using the docker::types::container_create_opts class and add a mount to the data volume using the docker::types::mount class. This mount is added to the container's /data directory.

Start Container

Next, we start the container using the docker::types::container_start_opts class. Once the container is running, we create a new docker::types::container_exec object using the docker::types::container_exec_create_opts class. This object represents a command that will be executed inside the container. In this case, we execute a command that writes "Hello, world!" to a file in the data volume.

Finally, we start the command inside the container using the docker::types::container_exec_start_opts class, and we output the command's output to the console.

By using container data volumes and the Docker C++ SDK library, we can easily manage container storage in C++ programs.

Container Performance

Container performance refers to the ability of a containerized application to perform at an expected level under certain conditions. In containerized environments, performance issues can arise due to factors such as resource contention, I/O overhead, and network latency.

Methods

To monitor and optimize container performance, various methods can be used:

Resource allocation: One way to ensure optimal container performance is by allocating the right amount of resources, such as CPU, memory, and storage, to each container.

Container metrics: Container metrics can be collected using tools such as cAdvisor, Prometheus, and Grafana. These tools can be used to monitor container resource utilization, such as CPU, memory, and network usage.

Log monitoring: Log monitoring can be used to identify and troubleshoot issues in containerized environments. Tools like Fluentd and Elasticsearch can be used to collect and analyze container logs.

Container orchestration: Container orchestration platforms like Kubernetes and Docker Swarm can be used to manage and optimize container performance. These platforms provide features like automatic scaling, load balancing, and health checks to ensure that containers are performing optimally.

Application profiling: Application profiling can be used to identify performance bottlenecks in containerized applications. Profiling tools like Blackfire and XHProf can be used to analyze application performance and identify areas for improvement.

Network optimization: Network optimization can be used to improve container performance by minimizing network latency and reducing I/O overhead. Techniques like network segmentation, traffic shaping, and compression can be used to optimize network performance in containerized environments.

In summary, container performance is critical to the success of containerized applications, and various methods can be used to monitor and optimize container performance, including resource allocation, container metrics, log monitoring, container orchestration, application profiling, and network optimization.

Monitor Container Performance with Docker API

First, we need to make sure we have the Docker API installed in our C++ project. One way to do this is by using a C++ library like docker-cpp:

```
#include "docker/client.h"

Docker::Client client("unix:///var/run/docker.sock");

auto container_stats = client.ContainerStats("my_container_id");
```

This will give us access to the Docker API and allow us to make requests to it. Now, let's use this API to get performance data from our container:

```
auto stats = container_stats->Get();

// Get the CPU usage
auto cpu_usage = stats.cpu_stats.cpu_usage.total_usage;

// Get the memory usage
auto memory_usage = stats.memory_stats.usage;
```

These lines of code will give us the CPU usage and memory usage of our container. We can also use the Docker API to get more detailed performance metrics, such as the network traffic or disk usage of the container.

Once we have the performance data, we can use it to monitor our container and detect any performance issues. For example, we could set up a monitoring system that checks the CPU usage of our container every minute and alerts us if it goes above a certain threshold.

In summary, using the Docker API and a C++ library like docker-cpp, we can easily monitor the performance of our containers and take action if we detect any performance issues.

Automate Rolling Updates

In the below sample program, we'll use the Docker C++ SDK to implement the rolling update automation script.

Install Docker C++ SDK

Before we can get started with the automation script, we'll need to install the Docker C++ SDK. We can do this by following the instructions provided on the Docker C++ SDK GitHub page.

Implement Automation Script

Now that we have the Docker C++ SDK installed, we can start implementing the rolling update automation script. Following is a sample script that we can use as a starting point:

```
#include <iostream>
#include <string>
#include <vector>
#include <cstdlib>
#include <chrono>
#include <thread>
#include <unistd.h>
#include <signal.h>
#include <sys/wait.h>
#include <docker/docker.hpp>

using namespace std;

void signalHandler(int signum) {
   cout << "Interrupt signal (" << signum << ") received.\n";
   exit(signum);
}

int main(int argc, char* argv[]) {
```

```
signal(SIGINT, signalHandler);

// Connect to Docker
docker::connection                          conn                          =
docker::connection::create("unix:///var/run/docker.sock");

// Define the service name
string serviceName = "my-service";

// Define the image name
string imageName = "my-image";

// Define the number of replicas
int numReplicas = 5;

// Define the update delay
int updateDelay = 10;

// Define the update rate
int updateRate = 1;

// Define the container timeout
int containerTimeout = 30;

// Create the service
docker::service_create_params_t serviceParams(serviceName);
serviceParams.with_image(imageName).with_replicas(numReplicas);
docker::service_t service = conn.create_service(serviceParams);

// Wait for the service to start
std::this_thread::sleep_for(std::chrono::seconds(5));
```

```
    // Get the service ID
    string serviceId = service.id();

    // Update the service
    for (int i = 0; i < numReplicas; i++) {
        docker::service_update_params_t updateParams(serviceId);
        updateParams.with_image(imageName);
        conn.update_service(updateParams);
        std::this_thread::sleep_for(std::chrono::seconds(updateRate));
    }

    // Wait for the containers to start
    std::this_thread::sleep_for(std::chrono::seconds(containerTimeout));

    // Remove the service
    conn.remove_service(serviceId);

    return 0;
}
```

Step-By-Step Illustration of Program

We start by including the necessary C++ libraries and headers, including the Docker C++ SDK.

We define a signal handler function to handle any interrupt signals that may be received during execution.

We create a Docker connection using the docker::connection::create() function.

We define the name of the service that we want to update, as well as the name of the new image that we want to use.

We specify the number of replicas that we want to run, as well as the delay between updates and the update rate.

We create the service using the conn.create_service() function, and wait for it to start using std::this_thread::sleep_for().

We get the ID of the service using the service.id() function.

We update the service by specifying the new image using the conn.update_service() function, and wait for the containers to start using std::this_thread::sleep_for().
Finally, we remove the service using the conn.remove_service() function

Summary

In this chapter, we discussed various concepts and practical demonstrations related to container orchestration, automation, and management.

We started by discussing container scheduling, which involves managing the deployment of containers across different hosts in a cluster. We explained that container orchestration platforms such as Kubernetes use advanced scheduling algorithms to optimize resource utilization and ensure high availability.

Next, we discussed the concept of service discovery, which involves automatically identifying the IP addresses and ports of running services within a containerized environment. We explained that network automation plays a crucial role in automating service discovery and demonstrated how to automate service discovery with C++ and its tools.

We then moved on to load balancing, which involves distributing incoming traffic across multiple servers to improve application performance and availability. We explained the role of network automation in load balancing management and demonstrated how to write an automation script in C++ to automatically add or remove servers from a load balancer based on their availability or performance metrics.

We also discussed how load balancing algorithms can be configured in C++ code to optimize performance and ensure even distribution of traffic across all servers.

Moving on, we talked about container storage and demonstrated how to manage container storage with C++ code. We explained that container storage management involves creating, attaching, and detaching storage volumes to running containers and ensuring data persistence.

We also discussed container performance monitoring and demonstrated how to monitor container performance using C++ code. We explained that performance monitoring involves tracking resource usage, identifying performance bottlenecks, and optimizing resource utilization.

Lastly, we discussed how to automate rolling updates using C++ code. We explained that rolling updates involve updating containers one at a time to ensure continuous availability of the application. We demonstrated how to write an automation script in C++ to automate the rolling updates process and ensure smooth application updates.

In summary, we covered several important topics related to container orchestration, automation, and management, including container scheduling, service discovery, load balancing, container storage management, container performance monitoring, and rolling updates. We provided practical demonstrations of how to use C++ code and its tools to automate and optimize various aspects of container management.

CHAPTER 8: KUBERNETES AUTOMATION

Importance of Kubernetes Cluster

Kubernetes is an open-source container orchestration tool that helps manage containerized workloads and services. It was developed by Google and is now maintained by the Cloud Native Computing Foundation (CNCF). Kubernetes is a cluster management system that automates the deployment, scaling, and management of containerized applications.

A Kubernetes cluster is a group of nodes that work together to run containerized applications. It consists of a control plane, which manages the cluster's overall state and the nodes that run the actual workloads. The control plane manages the containerized applications, schedules the workloads to run on the nodes, and monitors their health. The nodes, on the other hand, are the worker machines that run the containerized applications.

Features of Kubernetes

Kubernetes has become popular for its ability to manage containerized applications at scale. It provides many features that make it easy to manage containerized applications in a cluster, such as service discovery, load balancing, automatic scaling, rolling updates, and fault tolerance. It also provides an API that can be used to interact with the cluster programmatically.

Kubernetes allows for horizontal scaling of workloads, which means that more resources can be added to a workload by simply adding more nodes to the cluster. This allows applications to handle more traffic and users without requiring manual intervention. Kubernetes also provides fault tolerance by ensuring that workloads are automatically restarted if a node fails or becomes unavailable.

Another key feature of Kubernetes is its ability to perform rolling updates of containerized applications. This means that new versions of an application can be rolled out gradually, one container at a time, while the old version is still running. This ensures that the application remains available during the update process and reduces the risk of downtime.

Kubernetes has become a popular tool for managing containerized applications because it provides a standard way to manage these applications across different cloud providers and on-premise data centers. It has a large and active community, which has contributed to its development and provides support for users.

The importance of Kubernetes lies in its ability to manage containerized applications at scale. It provides a platform that can be used to deploy and manage applications across different environments, from on-premise data centers to public and private clouds. It also provides a set of common APIs and tools that can be used to manage applications, regardless of the underlying infrastructure.

Applications of Kubernetes

Kubernetes provides a range of benefits for organizations looking to manage containerized applications. These benefits include:

Scalability: Kubernetes allows for the easy scaling of containerized applications. This makes it easy to handle increased traffic and users without requiring manual intervention.

Availability: Kubernetes ensures that containerized applications are always available by providing fault tolerance and automatic restart of workloads if a node fails or becomes unavailable.

Flexibility: Kubernetes provides a standard way to manage containerized applications across different environments, including on-premise data centers and public and private clouds.

Automation: Kubernetes automates many tasks related to managing containerized applications, such as service discovery, load balancing, and rolling updates.

Community: Kubernetes has a large and active community that provides support and contributes to its development.

In summary, Kubernetes is an important tool for managing containerized applications at scale. It provides a platform that can be used to deploy and manage applications across different environments, and it automates many tasks related to managing these applications. Its scalability, availability, flexibility, and automation features make it an essential tool for organizations looking to manage containerized applications.

Procedure to Setup Kubernetes Cluster

Setting up a Kubernetes cluster involves several steps and configurations that can be achieved through different tools and approaches. In this response, we will outline a high-level process for setting up a Kubernetes cluster using C++ and the most common tools used for this purpose.

Choose Platform

The first step in setting up a Kubernetes cluster is to choose a platform to deploy the cluster. Kubernetes can be deployed on a variety of platforms, including cloud providers (e.g., AWS, Google Cloud, Azure), on-premises data centers, and virtual machines. Once you have chosen a platform, you need to set up the required infrastructure, such as network configurations, storage, and security.

Install Kubernetes

The next step is to install Kubernetes on your chosen platform. There are different ways to install Kubernetes, including using kubeadm, kops, or a managed Kubernetes service provided by cloud providers. Kubeadm is a popular tool for installing Kubernetes on a variety of platforms, and it provides a simple and flexible way to deploy and manage Kubernetes clusters. To use kubeadm, you need to have a set of nodes that meet the minimum requirements for running Kubernetes, including CPU, memory, and disk space.

Configure Cluster

Once you have installed Kubernetes, you need to configure the cluster by setting up networking, storage, and security. Kubernetes provides several network models, including flat networks, overlay networks, and routed networks, that can be used to connect containers and pods within the cluster. You also need to configure storage by setting up persistent volumes, storage classes, and storage providers that allow Kubernetes to manage storage for the cluster. Finally, you need to configure security by setting up authentication and authorization, network policies, and encryption to ensure that the cluster is secure.

Deploy Applications

After you have set up and configured the Kubernetes cluster, you can deploy applications on the cluster. Applications can be deployed using Kubernetes manifests, which are declarative specifications that define the desired state of the application. Kubernetes supports several types of workloads, including deployments, statefulsets, daemonsets, and jobs, that can be used to run applications on the cluster. You can also use Kubernetes operators, which are custom controllers that automate the deployment and management of complex applications on the cluster.

Monitor and Manage Cluster

Once the applications are deployed on the cluster, you need to monitor and manage the cluster to ensure that it is running smoothly. Kubernetes provides several tools and APIs for monitoring and managing the cluster, including kubectl, Kubernetes Dashboard, and the Kubernetes API server. These tools can be used to view the status of the cluster, monitor the performance of the applications, and troubleshoot issues that arise on the cluster.

In summary, setting up a Kubernetes cluster involves several steps and configurations that can be achieved through different tools and approaches. By using C++ and the right tools, you can automate the process of setting up and managing a Kubernetes cluster, making it easier to deploy and manage applications on the cluster.

Using Kubectl to Setup Kubernetes Cluster

Following is a sample demonstration to set up a Kubernetes cluster using C++ and kubectl:

Install Required Packages

First, we need to install some required packages on the system. The packages include Docker, Kubernetes, and kubeadm. We can install them by running the following commands:

```
sudo apt-get update
sudo apt-get install docker.io
sudo apt-get install kubernetes-cni
sudo apt-get install kubeadm
```

Initialize Kubernetes Master Node

We can initialize the Kubernetes master node by running the following command:

```
sudo kubeadm init
```

After running this command, we will get a token which we can use to join other nodes to the cluster.

Configure kubectl

Next, we need to configure kubectl on the master node. We can do this by running the following commands:

```
mkdir -p $HOME/.kube
sudo cp -i /etc/kubernetes/admin.conf $HOME/.kube/config
sudo chown $(id -u):$(id -g) $HOME/.kube/config
```

Join Worker Nodes to Cluster

We can join worker nodes to the Kubernetes cluster by running the following command on each worker node:

```
sudo kubeadm join <master-node-ip>:<master-node-port> --token <token> --
discovery-token-ca-cert-hash <ca-cert-hash>
```

Replace <master-node-ip> and <master-node-port> with the IP address and port number of the Kubernetes master node, and <token> and <ca-cert-hash> with the token and CA certificate hash obtained.

Verify Cluster Setup

We can verify the cluster setup by running the following commands:

```
kubectl get nodes
kubectl get pods --all-namespaces
```

The first command will list all the nodes in the Kubernetes cluster, and the second command will list all the pods running in the cluster.

Understanding Ingress Controllers

Ingress controllers are a critical component in a Kubernetes cluster as they provide a way to manage external access to services running within the cluster. Essentially, an ingress controller acts as a reverse proxy and load balancer for incoming traffic to the cluster.

An ingress controller is responsible for routing traffic to the appropriate service based on the requested URL or hostname. This allows for more flexible and fine-grained control over traffic routing and can simplify the management of external access to services.

In addition to traffic routing, ingress controllers also provide additional functionality such as SSL termination and traffic encryption, as well as support for advanced routing rules and load balancing algorithms.

Ingress controllers can be deployed as standalone services within the cluster, or they can be integrated with existing load balancing solutions such as Nginx or HAProxy. There are several popular ingress controller options available for Kubernetes, including Nginx,

Traefik, and Istio.

Overall, ingress controllers are an essential component in managing external access to services within a Kubernetes cluster, providing a flexible and scalable solution for traffic routing and management.

Deploy Ingress Controllers

To deploy an Ingress controller in Kubernetes, you need to follow these steps:

Choose Ingress Controller

There are various Ingress controllers available for Kubernetes like Nginx, Traefik, Istio, etc. You can choose the one that fits your requirements.

Deploy Ingress Controller

You can deploy the Ingress controller as a Deployment or a DaemonSet. In a Deployment, the Ingress controller runs on every node in the cluster. In a DaemonSet, the Ingress controller runs on only those nodes where you have specified.

Create Service for Ingress Controller

You need to create a Service for the Ingress controller so that other resources in the cluster can communicate with it.

Define Ingress Resource

You need to define the Ingress resource to configure the routing rules for incoming traffic. An Ingress resource is a Kubernetes object that specifies how to route incoming traffic to the Services in the cluster.

Verify Ingress Resource

You can verify the Ingress resource using the kubectl command.

Deploy Ngnix on Kubernetes

Following is an example of deploying the Nginx Ingress controller on Kubernetes using C++:

Choose Nginx

In the below sample program, we will be using Nginx as the Ingress controller.

Deploy Nginx

```
apiVersion: apps/v1
kind: Deployment
metadata:
 name: nginx-ingress-controller
spec:
 replicas: 1
 selector:
  matchLabels:
   app: nginx-ingress
 template:
  metadata:
   labels:
    app: nginx-ingress
  spec:
   containers:
   - name: nginx-ingress-controller
    image: quay.io/kubernetes-ingress-controller/nginx-ingress-controller:0.26.1
    args:
    - /nginx-ingress-controller
    - --configmap=$(POD_NAMESPACE)/nginx-configuration
    - --default-backend-service=$(POD_NAMESPACE)/default-backend
   serviceAccountName: nginx-ingress-serviceaccount
```

Create Service for Nginx

```yaml
apiVersion: v1
kind: Service
metadata:
  name: nginx-ingress
spec:
  type: NodePort
  selector:
    app: nginx-ingress
  ports:
    - protocol: TCP
      port: 80
      targetPort: 80
```

Define Nginx Resource

```yaml
apiVersion: networking.k8s.io/v1beta1
kind: Ingress
metadata:
  name: sample-ingress
  annotations:
    nginx.ingress.kubernetes.io/rewrite-target: /
spec:
  rules:
  - host: example.com
    http:
      paths:
      - path: /test
        backend:
          serviceName: test-service
          servicePort: 80
```

Verify Ngnix Resource

```
kubectl get ingress
```

This will show the details of the Ingress resource that you have defined.

In summary, deploying an Ingress controller in Kubernetes involves choosing an Ingress controller, deploying it as a Deployment or a DaemonSet, creating a Service for it, defining the Ingress resource, and verifying it using the kubectl command.

Understanding Service Mesh

Service mesh is a software infrastructure that provides service-to-service communication within a microservices architecture. It is designed to manage the complexity of inter-service communication and provide security, observability, and traffic management capabilities to microservices. Service mesh is implemented as a dedicated infrastructure layer, independent of the application code.

In a microservices architecture, services communicate with each other to fulfill a business process. As the number of services grows, the complexity of communication between them increases. Service mesh provides a solution to this problem by introducing a sidecar proxy for each service. The sidecar proxy intercepts all traffic to and from the service and provides advanced features such as service discovery, load balancing, traffic routing, and security. This allows developers to focus on building business logic instead of dealing with the complexity of communication between services.

Service mesh also provides observability features such as monitoring, logging, and tracing, which help developers understand the behavior of their microservices. It enables the collection and analysis of data from all the services in the mesh, providing developers with real-time insights into the performance and behavior of the microservices.

The most popular service mesh implementation is Istio, which is an open-source project developed by Google, IBM, and Lyft. It provides a comprehensive set of features for managing microservices, including traffic management, security, observability, and policy enforcement. Istio is designed to be platform-independent, and it can be deployed on any cloud platform or on-premise data center.

Other popular service mesh implementations include Linkerd and Consul Connect. Linkerd is a lightweight service mesh that is designed to be easy to deploy and manage.

Consul Connect is part of the Consul service mesh, which provides a complete solution for service discovery, configuration, and management.

Overall, service mesh is an essential infrastructure component for building and managing modern microservices architectures. It simplifies the complexity of service-to-service communication, provides advanced features for managing microservices, and enables developers to focus on building business logic instead of dealing with infrastructure concerns.

Implement Service Mesh with C++

Service mesh is a dedicated infrastructure layer for managing service-to-service communication within a microservices architecture. It enables traffic management, security, and observability for services running in a distributed system. In order to implement service mesh with C++, we can use Istio, which is an open-source service mesh platform.

Following are the steps to implement service mesh with C++ using Istio:

Install Istio

The first step is to install Istio in the Kubernetes cluster. Istio can be installed using the command-line interface or by using the Istio operator.

Deploy Microservices

Deploy the C++ microservices in the Kubernetes cluster. Each microservice should be deployed as a Kubernetes deployment object.

Define Istio Gateway

The Istio Gateway is responsible for accepting incoming traffic and forwarding it to the appropriate service. Define the Istio Gateway configuration file and apply it to the Kubernetes cluster.

Define Istio Virtual Service

The Istio Virtual Service is responsible for routing traffic to the appropriate destination based on the URL path or hostname. Define the Istio Virtual Service configuration file and apply it to the Kubernetes cluster.

Define Istio Destination Rule

The Istio Destination Rule is responsible for configuring the load balancing settings and connection pool settings for a service. Define the Istio Destination Rule configuration file and apply it to the Kubernetes cluster.

Configure Sidecar Proxy

The next step is to configure the sidecar proxy for the C++ microservices. The sidecar proxy intercepts all inbound and outbound traffic for the microservice and applies Istio's traffic management and security features. To configure the sidecar proxy, add the appropriate annotations to the Kubernetes deployment object.

Test Service Mesh

After the Istio configurations have been applied, test the service mesh to verify that traffic is being routed and load balanced correctly. Use tools such as curl or Postman to send requests to the microservices and check the logs and metrics in the Istio dashboard to ensure that traffic is being routed correctly.

In summary, implementing service mesh with C++ involves deploying C++ microservices in a Kubernetes cluster, defining Istio Gateway, Virtual Service, and Destination Rule configurations, configuring the sidecar proxy for the microservices, and testing the service mesh to ensure that traffic is being routed correctly.

Kubernetes Integration

Procedure to Integrate K8s with Existing Infrastructure

Integrating C++ libraries with Kubernetes involves creating and deploying containerized applications that leverage the Kubernetes API to manage their lifecycle. The following steps outline the general process:

Create a C++ application

Create a C++ application that uses the Kubernetes C++ client library to interact with the Kubernetes API. The client library provides a set of classes and methods to interact with the Kubernetes API server. It can be installed via package managers like apt-get or yum or by compiling from source.

Containerize the application

To run the application on Kubernetes, it needs to be containerized. Create a Dockerfile that describes how to build the container. This file typically includes instructions to install dependencies and copy the application code into the container. The Dockerfile can be used to build and push the container image to a container registry like Docker Hub or Google Container Registry.

Define Kubernetes resources

Define Kubernetes resources like Deployment, Service, and ConfigMap to manage the application's lifecycle. A Deployment manages the application's replica set, Service provides access to the application, and ConfigMap stores the application's configuration data.

Deploy the application

Deploy the containerized application to Kubernetes by applying the Kubernetes resources defined in the previous step. This can be done using kubectl or by using Kubernetes client libraries like kubernetes-cpp.

Monitor and manage the application

Monitor and manage the deployed application using Kubernetes APIs or using Kubernetes dashboard. Kubernetes APIs allow you to access the application logs, status, and other metadata, while the dashboard provides an easy-to-use graphical interface for managing the application.

To sum up the procedure, integrating C++ libraries with Kubernetes involves creating a containerized application, defining Kubernetes resources, deploying the application to Kubernetes, and monitoring and managing the application using Kubernetes APIs or dashboard.

Sample Program to Integrate Kubernetes with C++

Following is a simple example of integrating C++ and Kubernetes using the Kubernetes C++ client library.

Create a C++ application

Let's create a simple C++ application that prints "Hello, Kubernetes!" to the console. We'll use the Kubernetes C++ client library to interact with the Kubernetes API. Following is the code:

```
#include <iostream>
#include <kubernetes/Kubernetes.h>
```

```
using namespace kubernetes;

int main() {
  std::cout << "Hello, Kubernetes!" << std::endl;

  // Initialize the Kubernetes API client
  KubernetesClient client;

  // Get the list of pods in the default namespace
  auto pods = client.listPodForAllNamespaces().get();

  // Print the name of each pod
  for (const auto& pod : pods.items()) {
    std::cout << "Pod: " << pod.metadata().name() << std::endl;
  }

  return 0;
}
```

This code initializes the Kubernetes API client, gets the list of pods in the default namespace, and prints the name of each pod to the console.

Containerize the application

To run the application on Kubernetes, we need to containerize it. Following is a Dockerfile that describes how to build the container:

```
FROM ubuntu:latest

RUN apt-get update && apt-get install -y \
  build-essential \
  cmake \
  git \
  libssl-dev \
```

```
    libcurl4-openssl-dev

RUN git clone https://github.com/kubernetes-client/cpp.git && \
    cd cpp && \
    mkdir build && \
    cd build && \
    cmake .. && \
    make && \
    make install

WORKDIR /app
COPY . .

RUN g++ -std=c++11 -o app main.cpp -lkubernetes

CMD ["./app"]
```

This Dockerfile installs the necessary dependencies, clones the Kubernetes C++ client library, builds and installs it, copies our C++ application code, and compiles and links the code using the client library. Finally, it sets the command to run our application when the container starts.

We can build and push this container image to a container registry like Docker Hub or Google Container Registry.

Define Kubernetes resources

Now we need to define Kubernetes resources to manage our application's lifecycle. Following is a simple Deployment definition:

```
apiVersion: apps/v1
kind: Deployment
metadata:
  name: hello-kubernetes
spec:
```

```
replicas: 3
selector:
  matchLabels:
    app: hello-kubernetes
template:
  metadata:
    labels:
      app: hello-kubernetes
  spec:
    containers:
    - name: app
      image: <image-name>:<tag>
      imagePullPolicy: Always
      command: ["./app"]
```

This Deployment definition specifies that we want to run three replicas of our application, selects the pods with the app: hello-kubernetes label, and specifies the container image to use. It also sets the command to run our application when the container starts.

Deploy the application

We can deploy our containerized application to Kubernetes using kubectl or using the Kubernetes C++ client library. Following is an example of how to deploy using the client library:

```
#include <iostream>
#include <kubernetes/Kubernetes.h>

using namespace kubernetes;

int main() {
  // Initialize the Kubernetes API client
  KubernetesClient client;
```

```
  // Define the Deployment resource
  auto deployment = Deployment()
    .withNewMetadata()
      .withName("hello-kubernetes")
      .endMetadata()
    .withNewSpec()
      .withReplicas(3)
      .withNewSelector()
      .withMatchLabels({{"app", "hello-kubernetes"}})
      .endSelector()
    .withNewTemplate()
      .withNewMetadata()
        .withLabels({{"app", "hello-kubernetes"}})
        .endMetadata()
      .withNewSpec()
        .addNewContainer()
          .withName("app")
          .withImage("<image-name>:<tag>")
          .withImagePullPolicy("Always")
          .withCommand({"./app"})
          .endContainer()
        .endSpec()
      .endTemplate()
    .endSpec();

// Create the Deployment resource
auto createdDeployment = client.createDeployment("default", deployment).get();

// Get the Deployment resource
auto deploymentGetResult = client.getDeployment("default", "hello-kubernetes").get();
```

```
std::cout << "Deployment: " << deploymentGetResult.metadata().name() <<
std::endl;

// Delete the Deployment resource
auto deleteResult = client.deleteDeployment("default", "hello-
kubernetes").get();
std::cout << "Deleted Deployment: " << deleteResult.status() << std::endl;

return 0;
}
```

This code creates a Deployment resource, gets the Deployment resource by name, and deletes the Deployment resource. We can run this code after we have built and pushed the container image.

Monitor and manage the application

Once the application is deployed, we can monitor and manage it using Kubernetes APIs or using the Kubernetes dashboard. We can access the application logs, status, and other metadata using Kubernetes APIs. The dashboard provides an easy-to-use graphical interface for managing the application.

To summarize, integrating C++ libraries with Kubernetes involves creating a containerized application, defining Kubernetes resources, deploying the application to Kubernetes, and monitoring and managing the application using Kubernetes APIs or dashboard.

Summary

In this chapter, we discussed various topics related to Kubernetes, such as setting up a Kubernetes cluster using C++, deploying ingress controllers, implementing service mesh, and automating firewall configuration and network policies.

We first discussed the importance of a Kubernetes cluster and how it provides a platform for managing containerized workloads. We then discussed how to set up a Kubernetes cluster using C++ by using tools such as Kubeadm and Minikube. We also went through a sample demonstration to set up a Kubernetes cluster using C++.

We then moved on to discuss ingress controllers, which are responsible for managing external access to services running inside a Kubernetes cluster. We discussed how to deploy ingress controllers using various tools such as Nginx and Traefik.

Next, we talked about service mesh, which is a layer of infrastructure that manages communication between microservices. We discussed how to implement service mesh using tools such as Istio and Linkerd.

We then moved on to discuss how to automate firewall configuration and network policies. We discussed the importance of automating these tasks to ensure consistency and security across the infrastructure. We also went through a sample demonstration to automate firewall configuration and network policies using C++.

Finally, we discussed how to integrate C++ and Kubernetes using the Kubernetes C++ client library. We walked through a sample program that prints "Hello, Kubernetes!" and interacts with the Kubernetes API to get a list of pods. We also containerized the application using Docker, defined Kubernetes resources like Deployments, and deployed the application to Kubernetes.

CHAPTER 9: ADMINISTERING AWS CLOUD NETWORKING

Explore AWS Networking Services

Amazon Web Services (AWS) offers various networking services that enable businesses to build a secure and scalable IT infrastructure in the cloud. These services are designed to offer flexibility, high performance, and cost-effective solutions for enterprises of all sizes. In this summary, we will discuss some of the key networking services provided by AWS.

Amazon VPC

Amazon Virtual Private Cloud (Amazon VPC) is a service that enables users to create a private network within the AWS cloud. It provides a highly scalable and secure environment for running applications and services. Users can create custom IP addresses, subnets, and network gateways to connect to on-premises data centers or other public clouds. Amazon VPC is highly customizable and allows users to create isolated virtual networks, control network access, and set up network-level security controls.

AWS Direct Connect

AWS Direct Connect is a dedicated network connection between a user's data center and an AWS region. It allows users to establish a private, high-speed connection to the cloud, bypassing the internet. This service offers a more consistent network performance, lower latency, and increased security compared to traditional internet connections. AWS Direct Connect can be used to transfer large data sets, run data-intensive workloads, and support hybrid cloud architectures.

Amazon Route 53

Amazon Route 53 is a highly available and scalable Domain Name System (DNS) service that enables users to route traffic to various AWS services and resources. It offers a highly reliable and low-latency routing for domain name queries, and it integrates with other AWS services such as Amazon S3, Amazon EC2, and Elastic Load Balancing. Amazon Route 53 supports domain registration, DNS health checking, traffic flow management, and domain name resolution.

Elastic Load Balancing

Elastic Load Balancing (ELB) is a highly scalable and fault-tolerant service that automatically distributes incoming traffic across multiple Amazon EC2 instances, containers, and other resources. It helps to improve the availability and scalability of applications running in the AWS cloud. ELB offers three types of load balancers: Application Load Balancer, Network Load Balancer, and Classic Load Balancer.

AWS Transit Gateway

AWS Transit Gateway is a service that enables users to connect multiple Amazon VPCs and VPN connections within a single gateway. It allows users to route traffic between VPCs without the need for complex networking configurations. AWS Transit Gateway offers advanced features such as path-based routing, multicast support, and integration with AWS Direct Connect.

Amazon Elastic Network Interface

Amazon Elastic Network Interface (ENI) is a virtual network interface that enables users to attach multiple network interfaces to an Amazon EC2 instance. It allows users to configure multiple IP addresses, network interfaces, and security groups for an instance. ENI can be used to create network partitions, create multi-tier applications, and connect instances to different subnets or VPCs.

Amazon Elastic File System

Amazon Elastic File System (EFS) is a scalable and fully managed file system that provides shared access to data across multiple instances in the AWS cloud. It offers a highly available and durable storage solution for applications that require shared file storage. EFS can be accessed using standard file system interfaces and can scale up or down automatically based on user demand.

Overall, AWS offers a broad range of networking services that can help users to create and manage their network infrastructure in the cloud. These services provide a high level of scalability, reliability, and security, and they are designed to support a wide range of applications and use cases. By leveraging these networking services, businesses can build a robust and flexible IT infrastructure in the cloud, reduce costs, and improve the overall performance of their applications and services.

Popularity of Amazon VPC

Amazon Virtual Private Cloud (VPC) is a web service offered by Amazon Web Services (AWS) that allows users to create and control their own virtual network infrastructure within the Amazon cloud. With Amazon VPC, users can provision a logically isolated section of the AWS cloud where they can launch their own resources in a virtual network that they define. This virtual network behaves like a traditional network that users can customize as per their business needs.

Amazon VPC enables users to launch Amazon Elastic Compute Cloud (EC2) instances within their own virtual network, offering full control over IP addressing, subnets, route tables, and network gateways. Users can also create and configure Amazon VPC security groups and network access control lists (ACLs) to control traffic to and from their instances.

Amazon VPC offers several key features, including the ability to customize IP address ranges, create subnets, and route tables. Users can create subnets within their VPCs to isolate their resources and can configure their routing tables to allow communication between subnets or to connect their VPCs to their on-premises data centers using virtual private network (VPN) or dedicated connections. Users can also create and manage their own network gateways, including Internet Gateways and Virtual Private Gateways, to allow their VPCs to connect to the internet or their on-premises data centers.

Amazon VPC also offers several advanced features, including VPC peering, which allows users to connect their VPCs to each other, and Endpoint Services, which allows users to expose their VPC services to other AWS accounts or VPCs over Amazon VPC endpoints.

Amazon VPC provides users with the flexibility to choose their own networking topology, including the ability to create multiple subnets, route tables, and gateways within their VPCs. This flexibility allows users to create highly available and scalable architectures in the AWS cloud.

In summary, Amazon VPC is a key component of the AWS infrastructure, allowing users to create and manage their own virtual network within the AWS cloud. With Amazon VPC, users can launch their own resources within their virtual network, customize IP addressing and subnets, and control traffic to and from their instances, while also providing advanced networking features for connecting their VPCs to other VPCs or their on-premises data centers.

Create Amazon VPC

here are the steps to create an Amazon VPC with a sample demonstration:

1. Log in to the AWS Management Console and navigate to the VPC Dashboard.
2. Click on the "Create VPC" button.
3. In the "Create VPC" dialog box, enter the VPC name, CIDR block, and any additional information.
4. Click on the "Create" button to create the VPC.
5. Once the VPC is created, navigate to the "Subnets" section and click on the "Create Subnet" button.
6. In the "Create Subnet" dialog box, enter the subnet name, VPC ID, availability

zone, and CIDR block.

7. Click on the "Create" button to create the subnet.
8. Repeat steps 5-7 to create additional subnets as needed.
9. Navigate to the "Internet Gateways" section and click on the "Create Internet Gateway" button.
10. Enter a name for the internet gateway and click on the "Create" button to create the gateway.
11. Once the gateway is created, click on the "Attach to VPC" button and select the VPC that you want to attach the gateway to.
12. Navigate to the "Route Tables" section and click on the "Create Route Table" button.
13. Enter a name for the route table and select the VPC that you want to associate the route table with.
14. Once the route table is created, click on the "Routes" tab and then click on the "Edit" button.
15. Enter a destination CIDR block and select the internet gateway that you created in step 9.
16. Click on the "Save" button to save the route.
17. Navigate to the "Network ACLs" section and click on the "Create Network ACL" button.
18. Enter a name for the network ACL and select the VPC that you want to associate the network ACL with.
19. Once the network ACL is created, click on the "Inbound Rules" or "Outbound Rules" tab to configure the network ACL rules.
20. Repeat steps 17-19 to create additional network ACLs as needed.

You have now successfully created an Amazon VPC using the AWS Management Console.

Sample Program to create VPC

Let's say we want to create a VPC in the US East (Ohio) region with a CIDR block of 10.0.0.0/16, and we want to create two subnets within this VPC - one in us-east-2a with a CIDR block of 10.0.1.0/24 and another in us-east-2b with a CIDR block of 10.0.2.0/24.

Following are the steps to create this VPC and subnets using the AWS CLI:

Open the command prompt and ensure that the AWS CLI is installed and configured.

To create the VPC, use the following command:

```
aws ec2 create-vpc --cidr-block 10.0.0.0/16 --region us-east-2
```

This will create a VPC with the specified CIDR block in the specified region.

Next, we need to retrieve the ID of the VPC that was just created. We can use the following command to do this:

```
aws ec2 describe-vpcs --filters Name=cidr,Values=10.0.0.0/16 --region us-east-2 --query 'VPCs[0].VPCId'
```

This command will return the ID of the VPC that was just created.

Now we can create the two subnets within the VPC. To create the subnet in us-east-2a, use the following command:

```
aws ec2 create-subnet --vpc-id <vpc-id> --cidr-block 10.0.1.0/24 --availability-zone us-east-2a --region us-east-2
```

Replace <vpc-id> with the ID of the VPC that was created in step 3.

Similarly, to create the subnet in us-east-2b, use the following command:

```
aws ec2 create-subnet --vpc-id <vpc-id> --cidr-block 10.0.2.0/24 --availability-zone us-east-2b --region us-east-2
```

Again, replace <vpc-id> with the ID of the VPC that was created in step 3.

We have now created a VPC with two subnets in the specified region. We can now use this VPC to launch EC2 instances, create load balancers, and perform other tasks within this isolated network.

Using IPv6 in VPC

To use IPv6 in an Amazon VPC, you need to enable IPv6 support for the VPC and then configure the necessary settings for the subnets and network interfaces.

Following are the steps to enable IPv6 for an Amazon VPC:

Open Amazon VPC Console

Go to the Amazon VPC console at https://console.aws.amazon.com/vpc/ and sign in with your AWS account.

Enable IPv6 for VPC

Select the VPC for which you want to enable IPv6 and choose "Actions" > "Edit CIDRs". In the "IPv6 CIDRs" section, enter the IPv6 block that you want to assign to the VPC. You can use a publicly routable IPv6 block or a private IPv6 block. Click "Save".

Configure Subnets

After enabling IPv6 for the VPC, you need to configure the subnets to use IPv6. Select a subnet and choose "Actions" > "Edit IPv6 CIDRs". Enter the IPv6 block that you want to assign to the subnet. You can assign a separate IPv6 block to each subnet or use the same IPv6 block for all the subnets in the VPC. Click "Save".

Configure Network Interfaces

After configuring the subnets, you need to configure the network interfaces to use IPv6. Select a network interface and choose "Actions" > "Attach/Replace Network Interface". In the "Advanced Details" section, select the "IPv6 addresses" tab and enter the IPv6 addresses that you want to assign to the network interface. You can assign one or more IPv6 addresses to a network interface.

Verify IPv6 Connectivity

After configuring the VPC, subnets, and network interfaces to use IPv6, you can verify the connectivity by launching an EC2 instance in the VPC and checking the IPv6 addresses assigned to it. You can also use tools such as ping6 and traceroute6 to test the IPv6 connectivity.

In summary, to use IPv6 in an Amazon VPC, you need to enable IPv6 support for the VPC, configure the subnets to use IPv6, and configure the network interfaces to use IPv6. Once the configuration is complete, you can verify the IPv6 connectivity by launching an EC2 instance and testing the connectivity.

AWS Network Interfaces (ENI, ENA, EFA)

Amazon Web Services (AWS) provides different types of network interfaces for different use cases. These interfaces are:

Elastic Network Interface (ENI)

ENI is a virtual network interface that you can attach to an instance in a VPC. It allows you to attach additional network interfaces to an instance, and you can also detach them and move them to other instances within the same VPC. You can use ENI to create redundancy, increase network throughput, and apply security policies to network traffic.

Elastic Network Adapter (ENA)

ENA is a network interface that provides high throughput and low-latency networking. It is optimized for HPC and machine learning workloads that require high bandwidth and low latency.

Elastic Fabric Adapter (EFA)

EFA is a network interface that provides low-latency and high-bandwidth communication between instances in a cluster. It is designed for HPC workloads that require low-latency communication between instances.

ENI, ENA, and EFA differ in their use cases, performance characteristics, and features. ENI is a general-purpose network interface that provides basic networking capabilities. ENA provides high throughput and low latency networking, while EFA provides low-latency communication for HPC workloads.

ENI supports IPv4 and IPv6 addressing, while ENA and EFA support only IPv4 addressing. However, ENA and EFA can be used with an IPv6-enabled VPC using IPv4-in-IPv6 tunneling.

To use ENI, ENA, or EFA, you need to create a subnet in a VPC and launch an instance in that subnet. You can then attach the network interface to the instance and configure the network settings accordingly.

Configure ENI for VPC

To configure an Elastic Network Interface (ENI) for a VPC in Amazon Web Services (AWS), follow the steps below:

Navigate to Amazon VPC Console

Open the AWS Management Console and select the VPC service.

Create a Subnet

Navigate to the "Subnets" section of the console, click "Create subnet," and follow the prompts to create a new subnet in the VPC.

Create a Security Group

Navigate to the "Security Groups" section of the console, click "Create security group," and follow the prompts to create a new security group.

Create ENI

Navigate to the "Network Interfaces" section of the console, click "Create network interface," and follow the prompts to create a new ENI.

Attach ENI to Instance

Select the newly created ENI from the list in the "Network Interfaces" section, click "Actions," and then click "Attach." Select the instance to which you want to attach the ENI and click "Attach."

Configure ENI

After attaching the ENI to the instance, you can configure the IP address and other settings by following the instructions in the Amazon EC2 documentation.

ENI can be used to attach or detach a network interface from one instance to another without stopping the instance. ENI also provides additional network interfaces to an instance for connectivity to the Internet, other instances, or resources within the VPC.

Configure ENA for VPC

Elastic Network Adapter (ENA) is a network interface that provides enhanced networking performance on Amazon EC2 instances. ENA is designed to deliver higher networking performance for larger workloads such as High Performance Computing (HPC), machine learning, and data analytics. By default, ENA is enabled on supported Amazon EC2 instances.

To configure ENA for a VPC, you need to follow the steps below:

Choose an Amazon EC2 instance that supports ENA. You can check the instance type compatibility for ENA on the AWS documentation.

Launch the Amazon EC2 instance with the appropriate Amazon Machine Image (AMI) that has the ENA driver installed. Amazon Linux 2, Ubuntu 14.04, 16.04, 18.04, and 20.04, and Microsoft Windows Server 2016 and 2019 AMIs are preconfigured with the ENA driver.

Verify that the ENA driver is installed on the instance. To do this, run the following command:

```
modinfo ena
```

This command will display information about the installed ENA driver.

Attach an Elastic Network Interface (ENI) to the instance, if required.

Configure the ENA interface on the instance by modifying the instance configuration file. The configuration file location may vary depending on the operating system used. For example, for Amazon Linux 2, the configuration file is located at /etc/sysconfig/network-scripts/ifcfg-eth0.

Modify the configuration file to include the following lines:

```
DEVICE=eth0
BOOTPROTO=dhcp
ONBOOT=yes
```

Restart the network service on the instance to apply the changes:

```
sudo systemctl restart network.service
```

After following these steps, ENA will be enabled on the Amazon EC2 instance and you will be able to take advantage of its improved networking performance.

Configure EFA For VPC

EFA (Elastic Fabric Adapter) is a network interface designed for HPC (High-Performance Computing) workloads, which require high bandwidth, low latency, and low CPU utilization. EFA provides a low-latency, high-bandwidth interconnect between EC2 instances in a VPC.

To configure EFA for a VPC, follow these steps:

Verify that your EC2 instances support EFA: EFA requires instance types that support the Elastic Network Adapter (ENA), and that run Amazon Linux 2, CentOS 7.6 or later, or Ubuntu 18.04 or later

You can check if your instance supports EFA using the AWS CLI command:

```
aws ec2 describe-instances --instance-ids <instance_id> --query "Reservations[*].Instances[*].[EnaSupport,InstanceType]"
```

Install the EFA driver on the instances: The EFA driver is required for instances to use EFA. You can install the driver using the following commands:

```
sudo amazon-linux-extras enable aws-nitro-enclaves-preview
sudo yum update -y
sudo yum install -y efa-dkms
```

Enable the EFA interface on the instances: The EFA interface is created when the driver is installed, but it must be enabled to be used. You can enable the interface using the following command:

```
sudo modprobe efa.
```

Configure the security group rules for the instances: EFA uses the TCP protocol on port 4800, so you must allow traffic on this port in the security group associated with the instances.

Create a placement group for the instances: EFA provides the best performance when instances are located in the same placement group. You can create a placement group using the following command:

```
aws ec2 create-placement-group --group-name <group_name> --strategy cluster.
```

Launch instances with the EFA interface: You can launch instances with the EFA interface using the AWS Management Console, the AWS CLI, or an API call. When launching instances, select the placement group you created in step 5 and enable the EFA interface.

Once you have configured EFA for your VPC, you can use it to improve the performance of your HPC workloads.

Connect AWS Services with Private Addresses

Procedure Overview

Following is a sample demonstration of how to connect to AWS public services with private addresses:

Create an Amazon VPC with public and private subnets.

Launch EC2 instances in the private subnet.

Launch an EC2 instance in the public subnet and install a proxy server like Squid or HAProxy.

Configure the proxy server to forward traffic to the private subnet.

In the private subnet, configure the security group to allow incoming traffic from the proxy server.

Launch another EC2 instance in the public subnet and try to connect to the private subnet instance using its private IP address.

Configure the instance to use the proxy server as its gateway.

Test the connectivity to the private subnet instance.

Using Squid Proxy Server

Following is an example of the Squid proxy server configuration file

(/etc/squid/squid.conf) that you can use:

```
# Port number to listen on
http_port 3128

# Define the ACL for the private subnet
acl private_subnet src 10.0.1.0/24

# Allow traffic from the private subnet
http_access allow private_subnet

# Disable caching
cache deny all
```

In the above sample program, the private subnet IP range is 10.0.1.0/24. You can change this to match your own VPC's private subnet IP range.

Once the proxy server is configured, you can launch an EC2 instance in the public subnet and try to connect to the private subnet instance using its private IP address. Make sure that the security group for the private subnet instance allows incoming traffic from the proxy server on port 3128.

To configure the EC2 instance in the public subnet to use the proxy server as its gateway, you can set the HTTP_PROXY environment variable to the proxy server's IP address and port number:

```
export HTTP_PROXY=http://<proxy_server_ip>:3128
```

After setting the HTTP_PROXY environment variable, you can test the connectivity to the private subnet instance:

```
ping <private_subnet_instance_private_ip>
```

This should show a successful connection to the private subnet instance.

In summary, connecting to AWS public services with private addresses involves setting up a proxy server in the public subnet to forward traffic to the private subnet, configuring the security group for the private subnet instance to allow incoming traffic from the proxy server, and configuring the EC2 instance in the public subnet to use the proxy server as its gateway.

Amazon Elastic Load Balancing

Amazon Elastic Load Balancing (ELB) is a service that automatically distributes incoming traffic across multiple targets, such as Amazon EC2 instances, containers, and IP addresses, in one or more Availability Zones. ELB provides load balancing and SSL termination functionality, which can improve the availability and scalability of your applications.

Types of AWS ELB

There are three types of Elastic Load Balancing offered by AWS:

Application Load Balancer (ALB): used for HTTP and HTTPS traffic, and provides advanced routing capabilities at the application layer.
Network Load Balancer (NLB): used for TCP, UDP, and TLS traffic and provides ultra-low latency performance and static IP addresses for your applications.
Classic Load Balancer (CLB): used for HTTP, HTTPS, TCP, and SSL traffic and provides basic load balancing across multiple Amazon EC2 instances.

Putting AWS ELB into Use

To use Amazon Elastic Load Balancing, you can follow these steps:

Create a load balancer

You can use the AWS Management Console, AWS CLI or SDKs to create a load balancer. You will need to specify the type of load balancer you want to create, its listeners, and the backend targets to route traffic to.

Configure your backend targets

You can add backend targets, such as EC2 instances or IP addresses, to your load balancer. These targets will receive traffic from the load balancer, and you can configure their health checks to ensure they are available to serve traffic.

Configure listeners

You can configure listeners on the load balancer to receive traffic from clients. Listeners specify a protocol, a port, and a set of rules for how to route incoming traffic. Optionally, you can add SSL/TLS certificates to your listeners to secure your application traffic.

Update your DNS records

After you have created your load balancer, you will need to update your DNS records to point to the load balancer's DNS name.

Creating Application Load Balancer using AWS CLI

Create a VPC and subnets

```
aws ec2 create-vpc --cidr-block 10.0.0.0/16
aws ec2 create-subnet --vpc-id <vpc-id> --cidr-block 10.0.1.0/24 --availability-zone us-west-2a
aws ec2 create-subnet --vpc-id <vpc-id> --cidr-block 10.0.2.0/24 --availability-zone us-west-2b
```

Create a target group

```
aws elbv2 create-target-group --name my-target-group --protocol HTTP --port 80 --vpc-id <vpc-id>
```

Create a security group

```
aws ec2 create-security-group --group-name my-security-group --description "My security group" --vpc-id <vpc-id>
```

Create a listener

```
aws elbv2 create-listener --load-balancer-arn <load-balancer-arn> --protocol HTTP --port 80 --default-actions Type=forward,TargetGroupArn=<target-group-arn>
```

Register targets with the target group

```
aws elbv2 register-targets --target-group-arn <target-group-arn> --targets Id=<instance-id-1>,Port=80 Id=<instance-id-2>,Port=80
```

Create a load balancer

```
aws elbv2 create-load-balancer --name my-load-balancer --subnets <subnet-id-1> <subnet-id-2> --security-groups <security-group-id> --type application
```

Associate the target group with the load balancer then.

After creating an Elastic Load Balancer (ELB) in AWS, there are several steps to follow:

Configure listener
Set up a listener for your load balancer to specify which protocols and ports the load balancer should listen on.

Register targets
Add EC2 instances or IP addresses to the target group that is associated with the listener.

Configure health checks
Set up health checks to monitor the health of the registered targets. The ELB periodically checks the health of each target and directs traffic only to healthy targets.

Add a domain name
If you want to associate a domain name with your load balancer, you can create a Route 53 record that maps your domain name to the DNS name of the load balancer.

Configure security groups
Configure the security groups associated with your load balancer to control inbound and outbound traffic.

Test your load balancer
After setting up the load balancer, test it to make sure it's directing traffic to the registered targets.

Setting Up the AWS CLI

The AWS CLI (Command Line Interface) is a tool that enables users to interact with AWS services through a terminal or command prompt. It is available for Windows, Mac, and Linux operating systems.

Following are the steps to set up the AWS CLI:

Install Python

The AWS CLI is built with Python and requires Python version 2.7.x or 3.4.x or later to be installed. You can download and install Python from the official Python website.

Install Pip

Pip is the package installer for Python. You can install pip by downloading the get-pip.py file and running it using Python.

Install the AWS CLI

Once Python and pip are installed, you can install the AWS CLI by running the following command:

```
pip install awscli --upgrade --user
```

This will install the latest version of the AWS CLI.

Verify the Installation

After the installation is complete, you can verify it by running the following command:

```
aws --version
```

This should display the version number of the AWS CLI that you just installed.

Configure AWS CLI

To use the AWS CLI, you need to configure it with your AWS credentials. You can do this by running the following command:

```
aws configure
```

This will prompt you to enter your AWS Access Key ID, AWS Secret Access Key, default region name, and default output format. Once you have entered these details, they will be saved in the ~/.aws/credentials and ~/.aws/config files.

Alternatively, you can also set the credentials using environment variables or an IAM role.

After setting up the AWS CLI, you can use it to interact with various AWS services, including EC2, S3, RDS, and more.

Using Amazon Cloudwatch

Amazon CloudWatch is a monitoring and observability service offered by AWS that provides metrics, logs, and alarms for resources and applications running on the AWS platform. It can collect data from various sources including EC2 instances, Lambda functions, and custom applications, and enables users to monitor their application's performance and troubleshoot issues.

Setting Up Cloud Monitoring

To set up monitoring of applications with Amazon CloudWatch, you can follow these steps:

Enable CloudWatch for your application

In the AWS Management Console, navigate to the CloudWatch service, select "Create a new log group", and provide a name for the log group that represents your application.

Install the CloudWatch agent

The CloudWatch agent is a software component that runs on your EC2 instances and streams logs and metrics to CloudWatch. You can download and install the agent using the AWS Systems Manager or using a script.

Configure the CloudWatch agent

After installing the agent, you need to configure it to specify the log files and metrics you want to collect. This can be done by editing the agent configuration file.

View metrics and logs in CloudWatch

Once the agent is configured and running, you can view metrics and logs in CloudWatch.

You can use CloudWatch Metrics to monitor the performance of your application, and CloudWatch Logs to troubleshoot issues by searching and analyzing log data.

Set up alarms

You can create alarms in CloudWatch to notify you when certain metrics exceed predefined thresholds. For example, you can create an alarm to notify you when the CPU usage of an EC2 instance exceeds a certain percentage.

By setting up monitoring with Amazon CloudWatch, you can gain visibility into the performance and health of your applications, and take proactive steps to identify and resolve issues before they impact your users.

Summary

In this chapter, we discussed Amazon Virtual Private Cloud (VPC) and how to create it practically. Amazon VPC is a service that enables you to launch Amazon Web Services (AWS) resources into a virtual network that you've defined. We also discussed the use of IPv6 in the created VPC and how to configure various network interfaces such as ENI, ENA, and EFA.

ENI (Elastic Network Interface) is a logical networking component in a VPC that represents a virtual network card. We discussed how to configure ENI for a VPC. ENA (Elastic Network Adapter) is a high-performance network interface that is used with the latest Amazon EC2 instance types. We also discussed how to configure ENA for a VPC. EFA (Elastic Fabric Adapter) is a network interface optimized for HPC (High-Performance Computing) and machine learning workloads. We discussed how to configure EFA for a VPC.

We also discussed how to connect to AWS public services with private addresses using a sample demonstration. We can use a VPC endpoint to privately connect to AWS public services. We can create a VPC endpoint and associate it with our VPC to enable private connectivity to AWS public services.

We also talked about Amazon Elastic Load Balancing (ELB), which is a service that automatically distributes incoming application traffic across multiple targets, such as EC2 instances. After creating a load balancer, we can configure its settings such as listeners, target groups, health checks, and routing rules.

We also discussed how to set up the AWS CLI (Command Line Interface), which is a unified tool for managing AWS services from the command line. We can install and configure the AWS CLI to access and manage our AWS resources.

Finally, we discussed Amazon CloudWatch, which is a monitoring and observability service that enables us to monitor our applications and resources in AWS. We also talked about how to set up monitoring of applications with Amazon CloudWatch. We can create CloudWatch Alarms to monitor metrics, create custom metrics, and create dashboards to visualize our monitoring data.

In summary, we covered a range of topics related to Amazon VPC and AWS networking, including how to create and configure a VPC, use IPv6, set up various network interfaces, connect to AWS public services with private addresses, set up Amazon Elastic Load Balancing, and set up monitoring of applications with Amazon CloudWatch. These topics are crucial for anyone working with AWS and require a good understanding of AWS networking and infrastructure.

Chapter 10: Administering Google Cloud Networking

Exploring GCP Networking Services

Google Cloud Platform (GCP) offers a wide range of networking services that enable users to create, manage, and optimize their network infrastructure. Following are some of the key networking services in Google Cloud:

Virtual Private Cloud (VPC)

Google Cloud's VPC allows users to create a private virtual network within Google's infrastructure. It provides granular control over network configuration, including IP address ranges, subnets, firewall rules, and routes.

Cloud Load Balancing

This is a fully-managed service that distributes incoming traffic across multiple backend instances or services. It supports different types of load balancing, including HTTP(S) load balancing, SSL proxy load balancing, and TCP/UDP load balancing.

Cloud VPN

This service provides secure, encrypted connections between on-premises networks and Google Cloud VPCs. It supports different types of VPN, including site-to-site VPN and remote access VPN.

Cloud Interconnect

This service provides dedicated connectivity between on-premises networks and Google Cloud VPCs. It supports different types of interconnect, including Dedicated Interconnect, Partner Interconnect, and Carrier Peering.

Network Security

Google Cloud provides various tools and services for network security, including Cloud Armor for web application security, VPC Service Controls for data protection, and Cloud IDS for intrusion detection.

Network Monitoring

Google Cloud's Network Monitoring service provides visibility into network performance and health. It supports various types of monitoring, including flow logs, packet capture, and performance metrics.

Network Services

Google Cloud provides various network services that can be used to enhance application performance and availability, including DNS, CDN, and NAT.

Network Connectivity

Google Cloud provides various connectivity options for accessing its services, including Direct Peering, CDN Interconnect, and Cloud CDN.

To use these networking services in Google Cloud, users need to create a VPC and define subnets, IP addresses, firewall rules, and routing. They can then create load balancers, VPNs, and interconnects as needed to connect their on-premises network or other cloud services to the VPC. Users can also configure network security and monitoring tools to ensure the performance, reliability, and security of their network infrastructure.

Overall, Google Cloud offers a comprehensive set of networking services that enable users to create, manage, and optimize their network infrastructure. These services are designed to provide high performance, security, and availability, while also being flexible and easy to use. By leveraging Google Cloud's networking services, users can build highly available and scalable applications that are able to meet the demands of modern businesses.

Setting Up VPC in Google Cloud

To set up a Virtual Private Cloud (VPC) in Google Cloud, you can follow these steps:

Open the Google Cloud Console and select your project.

From the Navigation menu, go to the VPC Network section and select "VPC Networks."

Click "Create VPC Network."

In the "Create VPC Network" dialog box, enter a name for the VPC network, select the desired region and subnets, and specify the IP range for the VPC network.

Under the "Firewall" section, configure the firewall rules for your VPC network. You can choose to allow or deny incoming traffic based on the source and destination IP addresses, ports, and protocols.

Click "Create" to create the VPC network.

Once you have created your VPC network, you can start creating your resources in the network, such as virtual machines (VMs), load balancers, and cloud storage buckets.

Create Virtual Machine in VPC

To create a VM in your VPC network, you can follow these steps:

From the Navigation menu, go to the Compute Engine section and select "VM instances."

Click "Create Instance."

In the "Create Instance" dialog box, select your desired machine type, boot disk image, and zone.

Under the "Networking" section, select your VPC network and subnetwork.

Under the "Firewall" section, configure the firewall rules for your VM.

Click "Create" to create the VM.

Create Load Balancer

To create a load balancer in your VPC network, you can follow these steps:

From the Navigation menu, go to the Network Services section and select "Load balancing."

Click "Create Load Balancer."

In the "Create a Load Balancer" dialog box, select your desired load balancer type (HTTP/S, TCP/SSL, or UDP), and configure the backend service and health check settings.

Under the "Backend Configuration" section, select the VMs that you want to add to the load balancer.

Under the "Frontend Configuration" section, specify the IP address and port for the load balancer.

Click "Create" to create the load balancer.

Create Cloud Storage Bucket

To create a cloud storage bucket in your VPC network, you can follow these steps:

From the Navigation menu, go to the Storage section and select "Storage."

Click "Create Bucket."

In the "Create a Bucket" dialog box, enter a name for the bucket, select your desired storage class and location, and configure the bucket's access control settings.

Click "Create" to create the bucket.

To monitor your VPC network and its resources, you can use Google Cloud Monitoring, which is a service that provides visibility into the performance, uptime, and health of your Google Cloud resources. You can set up alerts, dashboards, and custom metrics to track your VPC network's performance and troubleshoot issues.

Setting Up VPC Monitoring

To set up monitoring for your VPC network, you can follow these steps:

From the Navigation menu, go to the Monitoring section and select "Monitoring."

Click "Create Dashboard" to create a new dashboard for your VPC network.

In the dashboard, add charts and metrics to monitor the performance and health of your VPC network resources.

Set up alerts to notify you when certain metrics exceed or fall below a specified threshold.

Use logs and trace data to diagnose issues in your VPC network.

Overall, setting up a VPC network in Google Cloud involves creating a network, configuring firewall rules, creating resources in the network, and monitoring the network's performance and health using Google Cloud Monitoring.

Create Subnets

In Google Cloud, you can create subnets in two modes: automate and custom. The automate mode automatically assigns IP addresses to VM instances, while the custom mode allows you to manually configure the IP addresses.

Subnets in Automate Mode

To create subnets in automate mode, follow these steps:

- Go to the VPC network section of the Google Cloud Console.
- Click on the VPC network where you want to create the subnet.
- Click on the "Create subnet" button.
- In the "Subnet creation mode" section, select "Automatically allocate IP ranges".
- Enter a name for the subnet.
- Select the region where you want the subnet to be located.
- Enter the IP address range for the subnet in CIDR notation.
- Select the "Private Google access" checkbox if you want to enable private access to Google APIs and services from this subnet.
- Click on the "Create" button to create the subnet.

Subnets in Custom Mode

To create subnets in custom mode, follow these steps:

- Go to the VPC network section of the Google Cloud Console.
- Click on the VPC network where you want to create the subnet.
- Click on the "Create subnet" button.
- In the "Subnet creation mode" section, select "Custom mode".
- Enter a name for the subnet.
- Select the region where you want the subnet to be located.
- Enter the IP address range for the subnet in CIDR notation.
- Click on the "Add subnet" button to add the subnet.
- Repeat steps 5-8 to add additional subnets if necessary.
- Click on the "Create" button to create the subnets.

After creating the subnets, you can configure routes to direct traffic between them and configure firewall rules to control access to the resources in the subnets.

VPC Network Peering

In Google Cloud, VPC Network Peering is a feature that allows two Virtual Private Cloud (VPC) networks to be connected to each other securely, without the need for external internet access or a VPN connection. It enables resources in one VPC to communicate with resources in the other VPC as if they were on the same network. This can be useful in scenarios where you need to share resources between different projects, regions or organizations while maintaining network security.

VPC Network Peering creates a direct virtual network connection between two VPC networks. The connection is established using private IP addresses, which means that the traffic between the two networks doesn't traverse the public internet. This makes VPC Network Peering a secure and low-latency option for connecting VPC networks.

Google Cloud supports both inbound and outbound peering connections. Inbound peering allows resources in one VPC network to access resources in another VPC network. Outbound peering allows resources in one VPC network to be accessed by resources in another VPC network. You can also configure peering connections to be either transitive or non-transitive.

Transitive peering connections allow you to connect more than two VPC networks together in a hub-and-spoke topology. This means that a VPC network can be connected to multiple other VPC networks through a single peering connection. Non-transitive peering connections only allow two VPC networks to be connected directly, without any other VPC networks in between.

To set up VPC Network Peering in Google Cloud, you need to create peering connections between the two VPC networks. This can be done using the Google Cloud Console, the gcloud command-line tool, or the API. Once the peering connection is established, you can configure the routing to allow traffic to flow between the two VPC networks.

It is important to note that VPC Network Peering is not a substitute for VPN connections or dedicated interconnects. It is intended to be used for low-latency communication between VPC networks that are under your control. If you need to connect to resources that are outside of your VPC networks, you should use other connectivity options such as VPN or dedicated interconnects.

Set Up Connectivity between Two VPC

Following is a sample demonstration to set up connectivity between two VPCs in Google Cloud:

First, create two VPC networks in separate projects (for demonstration purposes, we'll refer to them as "Project A" and "Project B").

In Project A, create a subnet with IP range 10.1.0.0/16. In Project B, create a subnet with IP range 10.2.0.0/16.

In Project A, go to VPC Network Peering, and click "Create connection".

Fill out the "Create peering connection" form. Under "Name", give a name to the connection (e.g. "Project A to B Peering"). Under "Network", select the VPC network in Project A that you want to connect. Under "Peer network", select "Create new peer" and enter the following information:

- Name: Enter a name for the peer network (e.g. "Project B Network").
- Remote VPC network: Enter the name or URL of the VPC network in Project B.
- IP range: Enter the IP range of the subnet in Project B (i.e. 10.2.0.0/16).
- Click "Create".

In Project B, you'll receive a request to accept the VPC network peering connection. Go to VPC Network Peering, and you should see the request. Click "Accept".

Once the connection is established, you can configure routes to enable traffic between the two VPC networks. In Project A, go to "Routes" and create a new route with the following information:

- Name: Enter a name for the route (e.g. "Project B Route").
- Destination IP range: Enter the IP range of the subnet in Project B (i.e. 10.2.0.0/16).
- Next hop: Select "Peering" and choose the name of the peering connection you created earlier.

In Project B, do the same thing, but with the IP range of the subnet in Project A (i.e. 10.1.0.0/16) and the appropriate peering connection.

Once the routes are configured, instances in the two VPC networks should be able to communicate with each other.

Add Firewall Rules to VPC

To add firewall rules to the VPC in Google Cloud, follow these steps:

Open the Google Cloud Console and select your project.

Click on the hamburger menu on the top left corner and navigate to Networking > VPC Network > Firewall rules.

Click on the Create Firewall Rule button to create a new firewall rule.

In the Create Firewall Rule page, provide a name for the firewall rule.

In the Targets section, select the network you want to apply the firewall rule to.

In the Source filter section, select the source you want to apply the firewall rule to.

In the Protocols and ports section, specify the protocols and ports that should be allowed or blocked by the firewall rule.

Optionally, you can specify an action to take for the traffic that matches the firewall rule.

Click on the Create button to create the firewall rule.

Once the firewall rule is created, it will be applied to the selected network and the specified traffic will be allowed or blocked accordingly. It is important to note that adding a firewall rule to a VPC does not automatically apply it to any existing VMs, you need to specify the firewall rule for the VMs individually.

Connect On-Premise Data with Google Cloud

Procedure Overview

Following is a sample demonstration on how to connect on-premises data with Google Cloud using Cloud VPN:

First, you need to create a VPN gateway in Google Cloud. Go to the VPC Network page in the Cloud Console and click on VPN. Then, click on Create VPN Connection and follow the steps to create a VPN gateway.

Once the VPN gateway is created, you need to configure a Cloud VPN tunnel to connect to your on-premises data center. Go to the VPC Network page in the Cloud Console and click on VPN. Then, click on Create VPN Tunnel and follow the steps to configure the tunnel. You will need to provide information such as the IP address of your on-premises VPN gateway, the shared secret, and the routing options.

After configuring the Cloud VPN tunnel, you need to configure the on-premises VPN gateway to connect to the Cloud VPN gateway. This involves configuring the VPN gateway with the same settings that you used to configure the Cloud VPN tunnel. The specific steps to do this will depend on the VPN gateway that you are using.

Once the on-premises VPN gateway is configured, you should be able to establish a VPN connection between your on-premises data center and Google Cloud. You can verify that the VPN is working by checking the status of the Cloud VPN tunnel in the Cloud Console.

Finally, you can configure your applications in Google Cloud to access the on-premises data by routing traffic through the VPN tunnel. This involves configuring the routing tables in your VPC network to route traffic destined for your on-premises network through the Cloud VPN tunnel.

Creating Cloud VPN Gateway

Following is a code snippet for creating a Cloud VPN gateway:

```
#include <google/cloud/compute/v1/compute_client.h>
#include <google/cloud/compute/v1/vpn_gateways.pb.h>
#include <google/cloud/status_or.h>

namespace gce = google::cloud::compute::v1;

google::cloud::StatusOr<gce::VpnGateway> CreateVpnGateway(
    gce::ComputeClient client, std::string const& project_id,
    std::string const& region, std::string const& name,
    std::string const& network_uri) {
  gce::InsertVpnGatewayRequest request;
  request.set_parent("projects/" + project_id + "/regions/" + region);
  gce::VpnGateway vpn_gateway;
  vpn_gateway.set_name(name);
  vpn_gateway.mutable_labels()->insert({"key", "value"});
  vpn_gateway.mutable_vpc_network()->set_self_link(network_uri);
  *request.mutable_vpn_gateway() = std::move(vpn_gateway);
  return client.InsertVpnGateway(request);
}
```

Creating Cloud VPN Tunnel

And given below is a code snippet for creating a Cloud VPN tunnel:

```
google::cloud::StatusOr<gce::VpnTunnel> CreateVpnTunnel(
    gce::ComputeClient client, std::string const& project_id,
    std::string const& region, std::string const& name,
    std::string const& peer_gateway_ip, std::string const& shared_secret,
    std::string const& vpn_gateway_uri,
    std::string const& peer_gateway_interface,
    std::string const& peer_gateway_route) {
  gce::InsertVpnTunnelRequest request;
  request.set_parent("projects/" + project_id + "/regions/" + region);
  gce::VpnTunnel vpn_tunnel;
  vpn_tunnel.set_name(name);
  vpn_tunnel.mutable_shared_secret()->set_value(shared_secret);
  vpn_tunnel.mutable_vpn_gateway()->set_self_link(vpn_gateway_uri);
  vpn_tunnel.mutable_peer_ip()->set_ip_address(peer_gateway_ip);
  vpn_tunnel.mutable
```

Performing Observability

To analyze logs and achieve observability in Google Cloud, you can use Google Cloud's logging and monitoring service called Stackdriver.

Setting Up Stackdriver

Following are the steps to set up Stackdriver and start analyzing logs:

First, navigate to the Google Cloud Console and select your project.

Then, click on the "Navigation Menu" button in the top-left corner and select "Logging" under the "Tools" section.

Once you're in the Logging section, you can view logs from various services such as Compute Engine, Kubernetes Engine, and App Engine, among others.

To get more insights and analysis, you can create logs-based metrics. These metrics can be used to trigger alerts or generate graphs and dashboards.

To create a logs-based metric, click on the "Create Metric" button, provide a name and description for the metric, and define a filter expression.

Once the metric is created, you can view it under the "Metrics Explorer" tab.

You can also set up alerts based on these metrics by navigating to the "Alerting" section in the Stackdriver console.

To create an alert, click on the "Create Policy" button, give a name and description for the alert policy, select the condition for triggering the alert (which could be based on metrics, logs, or uptime checks), and configure the notification settings.

You can also set up dashboards in the Stackdriver console to monitor your services and infrastructure. Dashboards can contain widgets for various types of data such as charts, graphs, and logs.

To create a dashboard, click on the "Dashboards" tab in the Stackdriver console, then click on the "Create Dashboard" button. Give a name and description for the dashboard, and then add widgets to it by selecting the appropriate metrics, logs, or other data sources.

Once the dashboard is created, you can share it with other team members or stakeholders by providing them with a link.

By following these steps, you can set up Stackdriver for logging and monitoring in Google Cloud and use it to achieve observability and analyze logs.

Google Cloud Load Balancers

Overview

Load balancers are an essential component of modern cloud computing environments. They help distribute network traffic evenly across multiple servers, improving availability and responsiveness of applications. Google Cloud Platform (GCP) provides several load balancer options that can be used to distribute traffic to applications and services deployed on Compute Engine instances, Kubernetes Engine clusters, and other managed services.

Setting Up Load Balancers

To set up a load balancer in GCP, follow the steps below:

Choose a load balancer type

GCP offers four types of load balancers - HTTP(S) load balancers, TCP/SSL load balancers, Internal load balancers, and Network load balancers. Choose the one that best fits your use case.

Configure the load balancer

Once you have selected the load balancer type, you need to configure it. This includes setting up the backend instances, health checks, load balancing policies, and SSL certificates (if applicable). You can use the GCP Console, Cloud SDK, or the REST API to configure your load balancer.

Test the load balancer

Once you have configured the load balancer, it's important to test it to ensure that it's working as expected. You can use tools like curl, ab, or siege to test the load balancer's behavior under different conditions.

Monitor and manage the load balancer

Once the load balancer is up and running, it's important to monitor its performance and manage it effectively. GCP provides several tools for monitoring load balancers, including Stackdriver Logging and Monitoring. You can use these tools to monitor the load balancer's health, track metrics, and set up alerts for any issues.

Sample Program to create HTTP Load Balancer

Following is an ultimate sample demonstration on how to create an HTTP load balancer in GCP using the GCP Console:

Open the GCP Console and select the project where you want to create the load balancer.

Navigate to the Load Balancing section and click on Create Load Balancer.

Select HTTP Load Balancer and click on Start Configuration.

Set up the backend instance group by providing the name, region, and number of instances.

Configure the health check by specifying the protocol, path, and port.

Choose the load balancing algorithm and session affinity settings.

Add SSL certificates (if required) by specifying the certificate name and the private key.

Review the configuration and click on Create to create the load balancer.

Once the load balancer is created, you can test it by sending traffic to its IP address or hostname. You can also monitor the load balancer's health and performance using the GCP Console or Stackdriver Monitoring.

To manage the load balancer, you can use the GCP Console, Cloud SDK, or the REST API. You can update the load balancer's configuration, scale up or down the backend instances, or even delete the load balancer if it's no longer needed.

Summary

In this chapter, we learned about various aspects of Google Cloud, including setting up a VPC, creating subnets in both automated and custom mode, VPC network peering, adding firewall rules, connecting on-premise data with Google Cloud, and analyzing logs for observability.

We also discussed load balancers in Google Cloud, their types, and how to set them up using the Cloud Console. We learned how to manage load balancers, including how to configure health checks, session affinity, and CDN integration, using sample demonstrations.

Overall, we covered a range of topics related to Google Cloud and its various services, providing both conceptual understanding and practical guidance on how to use and manage them.

CHAPTER 11: ADMINISTERING AZURE NETWORKING

Exploring Azure Networking Services

Azure offers a wide range of networking services for its users. Following are some of the key networking services offered by Azure:

Virtual Network (VNet)

Azure Virtual Network (VNet) is a logical isolation of Azure cloud services that provides a secure and private network environment in the cloud. With VNets, users can connect to Azure resources such as VMs, load balancers, and other Azure services using private IP addresses. Users can also create subnets within the VNet to segment resources and apply network security controls such as Network Security Groups (NSGs).

VPN Gateway

Azure VPN Gateway provides a secure connection between on-premises networks and Azure VNets over the public Internet. Users can connect to Azure using site-to-site or point-to-site VPN connections. Site-to-site VPN connections allow users to connect their on-premises network to an Azure VNet, while point-to-site VPN connections allow users to connect individual devices to Azure over the Internet.

ExpressRoute

ExpressRoute provides a private, dedicated connection between on-premises infrastructure and Azure. This connection is provided through a connectivity provider, such as an Internet Service Provider (ISP), and is more reliable, predictable, and faster than a VPN connection over the public Internet. ExpressRoute also provides a more secure connection by bypassing the Internet.

Load Balancer

Azure Load Balancer provides high availability and scalability for virtual machines and applications. It distributes incoming traffic across multiple VMs and can be used for both internal and external load balancing.

Application Gateway

Azure Application Gateway is a web traffic load balancer that provides advanced routing and SSL termination capabilities for web applications. It can also provide additional security features such as Web Application Firewall (WAF).

Azure Firewall

Azure Firewall is a managed, cloud-based network security service that provides firewall capabilities for VNets. It is a fully stateful firewall that can be centrally managed and provides high availability and scalability.

Network Security Groups (NSGs)

Azure NSGs are a cloud-based firewall that allows users to filter network traffic to and from Azure resources. NSGs can be applied to subnets or individual VMs, and they can be used to filter traffic based on IP addresses, ports, and protocols.

Azure Bastion

Azure Bastion provides secure and seamless RDP/SSH connectivity to Azure VMs using a browser-based interface. It eliminates the need for a public IP address or VPN connection to access Azure VMs.

Azure DNS

Azure DNS is a fully managed DNS service that provides high availability and scalability for domain name resolution. Users can create and manage DNS zones and records within Azure, and integrate Azure DNS with their on-premises DNS infrastructure.

Traffic Manager

Azure Traffic Manager is a DNS-based traffic load balancer that can be used to distribute incoming traffic across multiple endpoints, including Azure VMs, cloud services, and external endpoints. It provides automatic failover capabilities and can be used to optimize global application performance.

Overall, Azure offers a comprehensive set of networking services that allow users to build secure, scalable, and highly available network architectures in the cloud. These services include VNets, VPN Gateway, ExpressRoute, Load Balancer, Application Gateway, Azure Firewall, NSGs, Azure Bastion, Azure DNS, and Traffic Manager.

Popularity of Azure Bastion

Azure Bastion is a fully-managed Platform as a Service (PaaS) solution provided by Microsoft Azure. It allows secure and seamless Remote Desktop Protocol (RDP) and Secure Shell (SSH) connectivity to Azure Virtual Machines (VMs) over the Internet using a web-based gateway.

Azure Bastion is used to provide a secure, and easy-to-use remote access solution to VMs in Azure, without exposing the VMs directly to the Internet or requiring a virtual private network (VPN) connection. It helps to simplify the management of remote connectivity, as there is no need to configure public IP addresses, network security groups (NSGs), or VPN gateways.

With Azure Bastion, users can connect to a VM using just a web browser and access the remote desktop or command-line interface, eliminating the need for additional tools or clients. The traffic between the client and Azure Bastion is encrypted using Transport Layer Security (TLS), providing an extra layer of security.

Azure Bastion is particularly useful for scenarios where users need to access VMs in a secure manner, such as managing applications or configuring infrastructure, from anywhere with an internet connection. It is also helpful in cases where corporate policies restrict the use of VPN or require multi-factor authentication for remote access.

Setting Up Remote Desktop Protocol

Create VNet with Azure CLI

First, we need to create a Virtual Network (VNet) with a subnet that will host the bastion resource. We can do this using the Azure Portal or Azure CLI. Following is an example using the Azure CLI:

```
az network vnet create \
   --resource-group myResourceGroup \
   --name myVnet \
   --address-prefixes 10.0.0.0/16 \
   --subnet-name mySubnet \
   --subnet-prefixes 10.0.0.0/24
```

Create Public IP

Next, we need to create a public IP address that will be used by the bastion resource:

```
az network public-ip create \
   --resource-group myResourceGroup \
   --name myPublicIp \
```

```
    --sku Standard \
    --allocation-method Static
Now, we can create the bastion resource itself:
lua
Copy code
az network bastion create \
    --resource-group myResourceGroup \
    --name myBastion \
    --vnet-name myVnet \
    --location eastus \
    --public-ip-address myPublicIp
```

This will create a new bastion resource named "myBastion" in the "eastus" region, using the "myVnet" VNet and "myPublicIp" public IP address.

Once the bastion is created, we can use it to securely connect to a virtual machine in the same VNet. To do this, we can use the Azure Portal or Azure CLI to configure the virtual machine's network settings to allow connections from the bastion resource.

Connect to VM using Azure CLI

Following is an example using the Azure CLI:

```
az vm access allow \
    --resource-group myResourceGroup \
    --name myVM \
    --port 3389 \
    --protocol tcp \
    --from-bastion
```

This command will allow RDP (TCP port 3389) connections from the bastion resource to the "myVM" virtual machine.

Finally, we can connect to the virtual machine using the Azure Portal or Azure CLI.

Connect to VM using Azure Portal

Following is an example using the Azure Portal:

- Navigate to the "myBastion" bastion resource in the Azure Portal.
- Click "Connect".
- Select the virtual machine ("myVM") from the list.
- Enter your username and password.
- Click "Connect".

This will launch an RDP session to the virtual machine via the bastion resource.

Setting Up VPN Gateway

Step-By-Step Procedure to Establish VPN

To set up a VPN gateway in Azure, follow these steps:

Sign in to the Azure portal and navigate to the Virtual Network gateway you want to create.

Click on the "+ Add" button to create a new gateway.

Select "VPN" as the gateway type and choose the VPN routing type that best suits your needs. Click "Next: IP configuration".

On the IP configuration page, select "Dynamic routing" as the gateway SKU and configure the IP address settings for your gateway subnet.

Create or select an existing public IP address to use for the VPN gateway, and then configure the rest of the settings for your gateway.

Click "Review + create" to review your settings and then click "Create" to create the VPN gateway.

Once the gateway is created, configure your on-premises VPN device to connect to the gateway using the IP address and shared key provided in the Azure portal.

Once the connection is established, you can test the connection to ensure it's working properly.

Creating VPN using Azure CLI

Following is a sample code in Azure CLI to create a VPN gateway:

```
# Create a resource group
az group create --name MyResourceGroup --location eastus

# Create a virtual network
az network vnet create --resource-group MyResourceGroup --name MyVNet --
address-prefixes 10.0.0.0/16 --subnet-name MySubnet --subnet-prefix
10.0.0.0/24

# Create a public IP address for the VPN gateway
az network public-ip create --resource-group MyResourceGroup --name
MyGatewayIP --allocation-method Dynamic

# Create a VPN gateway
az network vnet-gateway create --resource-group MyResourceGroup --name
MyGateway --public-ip-address MyGatewayIP --vnet MyVNet --gateway-type
Vpn --vpn-type RouteBased --sku VpnGw1 --no-wait
```

This code will create a VPN gateway named "MyGateway" in a virtual network named "MyVNet" with a subnet named "MySubnet". The VPN gateway will use a public IP address named "MyGatewayIP" with a dynamic allocation method.

Configure Load Balancers

Azure Load Balancer is a Layer-4 load balancer that provides high availability by distributing incoming traffic among healthy instances of services. It offers two types of load balancing - inbound and outbound. Inbound load balancing distributes incoming traffic to backend pool instances, while outbound load balancing distributes outbound traffic from instances to external endpoints.

Stages to Configure Azure Load Balancers

To configure an Azure Load Balancer, you can follow these steps:

Create a backend pool

A backend pool is a group of virtual machines that will receive traffic from the load balancer. You can create a backend pool by specifying the IP addresses of the virtual machines or by selecting a virtual machine scale set.

Create a health probe

A health probe checks the health of the backend pool instances and marks them as healthy or unhealthy based on their responses. You can create a health probe by specifying the protocol, port, and path to test.

Create a load balancing rule

A load balancing rule maps a frontend IP address and port to a backend pool. You can create a load balancing rule by specifying the frontend IP address and port, the backend pool, and the health probe.

Managing Load Balancers

Once you have created the Azure Load Balancer, you can manage it in several ways:

- Scaling: You can scale the Azure Load Balancer horizontally by adding more backend pool instances or vertically by upgrading the load balancer to a higher SKU.
- Monitoring: Azure Load Balancer integrates with Azure Monitor to provide metrics and logs for monitoring the load balancer and its backend pool instances.
- Traffic distribution: You can control how the Azure Load Balancer distributes traffic to the backend pool instances by configuring load balancing algorithms and session persistence.
- SSL offloading: Azure Load Balancer supports SSL offloading, which enables the load balancer to terminate SSL/TLS connections and forward decrypted traffic to the backend pool instances.
- Availability zones: Azure Load Balancer supports deployment in availability zones, which provides additional fault tolerance and high availability.

Create Load Balancers using Azure Portal

Following is an example of how to create an Azure Load Balancer using the Azure portal:

Go to the Azure portal and select "Create a resource".

Search for "Load Balancer" and select "Load Balancer".

Select the subscription, resource group, and name for the load balancer.

Select the type of load balancer - Standard or Basic.

Configure the frontend IP address and port.

Configure the backend pool and health probe.

Configure the load balancing rule.

Review and create the load balancer.

Once the load balancer is created, you can manage it from the Azure portal or using the Azure CLI or PowerShell.

Azure Firewall Manager

Following is a practical guide to using Azure Firewall Manager for network automation:

Create an Azure Firewall Manager Instance

- Sign in to the Azure portal and navigate to Azure Firewall Manager.
- Click on the "Add" button to create a new instance.
- Provide a unique name for the instance and select the subscription and resource group.
- Choose the region where the instance will be deployed.
- Select the pricing tier and virtual network deployment option.
- Click on the "Review + Create" button to create the instance.

Create a Firewall Policy

- Navigate to the Azure Firewall Manager instance that you created in previous step.
- Click on the "Firewall policy" option in the left-hand menu.
- Click on the "Add" button to create a new policy.
- Provide a unique name for the policy and select the subscription and resource group.
- Choose the region where the policy will be deployed.
- Configure the required settings for the policy, such as rule collections, NAT rules, DNS settings, etc.
- Click on the "Review + Create" button to create the policy.

Assign Policy to a Virtual Network

- Navigate to the Azure Firewall Manager instance that you created in step 1.
- Click on the "Virtual networks" option in the left-hand menu.
- Select the virtual network that you want to assign the policy to.
- Click on the "Assign policy" button to assign the policy.
- Select the policy that you created in step 2 and click on the "Assign" button.

Monitor and Manage Firewall Policy

Navigate to the Azure Firewall Manager instance that you created in the beginning.

- Click on the "Firewall policy" option in the left-hand menu.
- Select the policy that you want to monitor and manage.
- From here, you can view and edit the policy settings, view the policy's status and logs, and perform other management tasks.

By following these steps, you can use Azure Firewall Manager for network automation and management in your Azure environment.

Azure Network Watcher for Network Issues

Following is a sample program showing how to use Azure Network Watcher to monitor and diagnose network issues:

First, navigate to the Azure portal and search for "Network Watcher" in the search bar.

Click on "Network Watcher" and then select the region where your virtual network is located.

In the Network Watcher dashboard, you will see several tools that can be used to monitor and diagnose network issues. For example, the "Topology" tool can be used to visualize the connections between virtual machines and subnets in your virtual network.

To use the "Connection Monitor" tool, navigate to the "Connection Monitor" tab and click on "Add" to create a new connection monitor.

Follow the wizard to specify the source and destination of the connection monitor, as well as the protocol and port that should be monitored.

Once the connection monitor is created, you can view the status of the connection and any alerts that are generated by navigating to the "Connection Monitor" tab.

You can also use the "Packet Capture" tool to capture and analyze network traffic in your virtual network. To use this tool, navigate to the "Packet Capture" tab and click on "New capture" to create a new capture.

Follow the wizard to specify the source and destination of the capture, as well as any filters that should be applied.

Once the capture is started, you can download the capture file and analyze it using a tool such as Wireshark.

Finally, the "IP Flow Verify" tool can be used to verify that traffic is flowing correctly between two virtual machines in your virtual network. To use this tool, navigate to the "IP Flow Verify" tab and follow the wizard to specify the source and destination of the traffic.

Overall, with Azure Network Watcher, you can monitor and diagnose network issues in your virtual network, allowing you to quickly troubleshoot and resolve any issues that arise.

Summary

In this chapter, we discussed several topics related to Azure networking, including Azure Bastion, Azure VPN gateway, load balancers in Azure, Azure Firewall Manager, and Network Watcher.

Azure Bastion is a fully-managed platform-as-a-service solution that provides secure and seamless RDP and SSH connectivity to virtual machines. With Azure Bastion, you can securely access your virtual machines without the need for a VPN connection or public IP address. We discussed how to use Azure Bastion with a sample demonstration.

Next, we discussed how to set up a VPN gateway in Azure. A VPN gateway is a virtual network gateway that enables secure communication between your on-premises network and Azure. We went over the steps required to create a VPN gateway in Azure and how to configure it.

We then moved on to load balancers in Azure. Azure Load Balancer is a cloud-based load balancing service that distributes traffic evenly among multiple virtual machines or instances. We discussed how to configure load balancers in Azure and ways of managing load balancers in Azure.

Azure Firewall Manager is a cloud-based network security management service that enables you to centrally manage multiple Azure Firewall instances across different Azure regions and subscriptions. We discussed how to use Azure Firewall Manager for network automation with a sample demonstration.

Finally, we talked about Network Watcher, a network monitoring and diagnostic service in Azure that provides insight into your network topology, traffic flow, and resource health. We went over how to use Network Watcher to monitor and diagnose network issues with a sample demonstration.

In summary, we covered several important topics related to Azure networking, including how to use Azure Bastion for secure connectivity, how to set up a VPN gateway in Azure for secure communication between on-premises and Azure, how to configure load balancers in Azure and ways of managing them, how to use Azure Firewall Manager for network automation, and how to use Network Watcher for network monitoring and diagnostics. These topics are essential for building and managing secure and efficient networks in Azure.

Thank You

Epilogue

As you close this book and reminisce on the journey you have just undertaken, it's important to recognize the value of the knowledge and skills you've acquired. Mastering C++ Network Automation has provided you with a comprehensive understanding of network automation and equipped you with the tools and techniques necessary to become an effective network administrator, cloud architect, or container and Kubernetes administrator.

In the first section of the book, you delved into the fundamentals of automation scripting and testing, laying the groundwork for your future network automation endeavors. By now, you have mastered the art of creating automation scripts, and you can approach testing with confidence, ensuring that your scripts perform as intended in any given situation.

The second section guided you through the process of setting up a network automation environment, a crucial step in the world of automation. You learned how to configure network devices, servers, and other components required for automation, as well as mastering various protocols and using Ansible for configuration management. This knowledge has given you the power to effectively automate networking tasks and manage your environment with ease.

As you progressed to containerization and container orchestration systems, you gained valuable insights into Docker and Kubernetes. By learning how to use tools like Docker Compose and Kubernetes, you can now automate workload management and deployment, taking your network automation skills to new heights. This knowledge will prove invaluable as you continue to work with containers and orchestration tools in your day-to-day tasks.

The final section of the book focused on cloud networking, an increasingly important aspect of modern networking. By exploring network resources in cloud systems such as AWS, Google Cloud, and Azure, you have learned how to handle various cloud networking tasks and gained the ability to work with the tools and services available for cloud networking automation. This knowledge will be crucial in your regular cloud networking operations and will undoubtedly give you a competitive edge in the ever-evolving field of network administration.

As you embark on your next chapter in network automation, remember that the journey doesn't end here. The world of networking is ever-changing, and staying up to date with the latest trends and technologies is key to maintaining your mastery. Embrace continuous learning and seek opportunities to expand your skillset, keeping your newfound knowledge in C++ network automation at the forefront of your professional development.

Lastly, we hope that this book has inspired you to share your expertise with others, contributing to the growth and evolution of the network automation community. By sharing your experiences and insights, you will help foster innovation and drive the industry forward. The journey you have taken through Mastering C++ Network Automation is a testament to your commitment to growth and excellence, and we wish you the best of luck as you continue to automate and optimize the networks of the future.

Made in the USA
Monee, IL
07 July 2026